ASTRAL
PROJECTION FOR
BEGINNERS

A Complete Guide to Astral Traveling, Out Of Body
Experience and How To Achieve Peace Of Mind
Through Meditation and Mindfulness

Lisa Amado

TABLE OF CONTENTS

INTRODUCTION

Astral Projection For Beginners: Is It Possible?

However, some are more effective than others.

Some people will swear by the usual methods such as meditation or lucid dreaming in order to achieve an astral projection that leaves them feeling fulfilled and happy. In contrast, some people feel more comfortable relying on visualization to project their consciousness from their physical body into the astral plane so they can enjoy this experience without having to use any type of technique that might make them uncomfortable while awake.

In fact, even the other techniques are usually adopted from ancient mysticism or new age philosophy, which some people tend to avoid. Which is why visualization continues to grow in popularity. It can help those who want to astral project while they are awake because it does not make them feel uncomfortable, anxious or strange in any way.

The basics of astral projection for beginners begin with visualization and finding a quiet space and time when there is no distraction around.

This does make it easier to focus on the idea of leaving your physical body, and when you do, it's helpful to create a calm and soothing image of yourself looking back at your physical form from above. You can even choose to see yourself as a spirit who is floating upward or downward through the clouds.

You will probably find that you can hold this image for longer than when you are trying to look down at your body below, but while doing so, you should remember that just like any other mental activity it is not real. It's just an idea of yourself looking outside of your body from an outside perspective as you observe yourself in motion.

This means that whatever happens does not alarm you because there is nothing to be "alarmed" over.

But this does not mean that you should do nothing while outside of your body. You can always choose to check up on yourself and make sure everything is okay. In this way, you can see that your mind is still functioning properly even though your body is not present in the physical world.

You can do all of this without feeling any discomfort at all because your mind is still fully active and you are not feeling vulnerable, restricted or fearful in any way at all. You may even find that you can do some of these things while floating up above your body from time to time as a form of meditation.

But if you feel like astral projecting for beginners has become new to you after a series of experiences, then it will be best to start off slowly with just a few simple visualization techniques so you get used to the idea and begin to accustom yourself to it.

The best thing to do is to start off by staying in the same place for a few minutes each day and continue to try and visualize this activity without making you feel any different than when you are awake. Over time, you will probably find that your mind is able to maintain this simple exercise of floating up above your body with ease.

WHAT IS ASTRAL PROJECTION?

Astral projection is an umbrella term that describes the practice of astral travel, an out-of-body experience, or OBE. The word "astral" in this context means "related to stars and other heavenly bodies."

What does astral projection feel like?

Many people who have experienced astral projection describe the feeling of floating above their body and looking down at their physical self below. It can also feel like dreaming while awake, or as if you are watching a movie scene from someone else's perspective. Some people can control what they see and do during an experience. Others see images that aren't under their control.

What does it mean if I have a near-death experience?

People who have near-death experiences often describe floating above their body and looking down at their physical self below. It can also feel like dreaming while awake, or watching a movie scene from someone else's perspective. Many people who have had near-death experiences say they felt no pain, and some didn't realize they were dying at first. Some people who have had near-death experiences also report seeing bright lights, or meeting with deceased relatives or religious figures. Of those who report such experiences, about 6 percent believe they were in heaven during the experience.

What is remote viewing?

Remote viewing is an extrasensory perception (ESP) technique that involves seeing images, hearing sounds, or receiving information about a distant person, location, or object. Remote viewing is often used as a synonym for ESP and may also refer to the participation of an agent in some distant observation. Like other forms of ESP, it has been investigated by laboratory experiments and by field experiments.

What does it mean if I have past-life memories?

Many people who report having had past-life memories describe vivid experiences that feel just like memories from their current life. If you have such experiences, you are not alone; many other people have undergone these experiences as well.

What is retrocognition?

Retrocognition is an extrasensory perception (ESP) involving knowledge of historical events and facts that the person could not have known otherwise. It can be used to describe a type of "psychic archaeology," in which the person acquires knowledge about an object, place, or person from the past.

What is remote healing?

Remote healing is a type of psionic healing in which one or more healers attempt to stimulate a subject's nervous system at a distance without physical contact.

What are mediumship and channeling?

Mediumship is the communication of messages from beings on the astral plane. The term "channeling" refers to a modern-day version of mediumship in which communication with spirits or guides is most often done through a person called a channeler, who serves as a medium for this information. The term encompasses many practices around the world, but the most common is known as mental channeling. Mental channeling (or mental mediumship) involves the communication of messages received mentally—by hearing, seeing, feeling, or sensing them in some other way—while in a trance state.

What is precognition?

Precognition is an extrasensory perception (ESP) involving knowledge of future events that the person could not have known otherwise. It can be used to describe a type of "psychic prediction" in which the person acquires knowledge about an event that has not yet occurred, but will occur in the future.

What are parapsychological phenomena?

Parapsychological phenomena are abilities, processes, and occurrences that cannot be explained by current science in whole or in part. A parapsychologist is a scientist who studies these phenomena.

What is the difference between a medium and a psychic?

A medium is an individual who conducts, possesses, or stimulates communication with discarnate entities. A psychic is a person who claims to have paranormal abilities. A person claiming to have these abilities could be a prophet or prophetess, but such individuals usually do not use the title "medium." Many people are intuitive and can receive information without making use of expensive equipment. However, some have been given special training in this area by top-level professionals.

What is spiritual healing?

Spiritual healing includes both traditional and modern practices of healing through prayer that involve use of the power of God or sacred spirits to effect health on physical or mental levels.

Remote viewing involves seeing images, hearing sounds, feeling sensations, or receiving information about a distant person, location, or object. Remote viewing is often used as a synonym for extra-sensory perception (ESP) and may also refer to the participation of an agent in some distant observation. Like other forms of ESP, it has been investigated by laboratory experiments and by field experiments.

Astral projection is an umbrella term that describes the practice of astral travel, an out-of-body experience, or OBE.

The word "astral" in this context means "related to stars and other heavenly bodies." This experience can take place in the physical body or in an ethereal, nonphysical body called a spirit or subtle body. Astral projection is typically characterized as an experience of being "in" one's body and at the same time being "outside" and observing the body from a distance. Astral projection can be used to refer to out-of-body experiences induced by various means, but the term usually implies intentionally leaving the physical body with intention. Some people report feeling vibrations or a pulling sensation before their spirit leaves their bodies. Others report seeing themselves lying in bed from above, often viewing themselves as if watching a movie scene from another person's perspective.

What is clairvoyance?

Clairvoyance is an extrasensory ability to see what is not present to the senses or known through normal means. Clairvoyance was originally used to describe seeing things at a distance, but it can also be used to describe a number of other experiences including out-of-body experiences (OBEs) and near-death experiences (NDEs). In some cases, clairvoyant information seems to have been received from the use of extrasensory perception (ESP). Clairvoyant information can come in many forms: symbols, images, words or phrases, sounds, or colors.

What is telepathy?

Telepathy is an extrasensory perception (ESP) involving the exchange of information without physical contact or the use of conventional sensory means such as sight, hearing, smell, taste, or touch. It can be used to describe a type of "psychic communication" in which information passes from one person to another. Telepathy is distinct from psychokinesis and precognition because those processes involve thought alone without the presence of mind-to-mind contact. Telepathy has been investigated by laboratory experiments and by field experiments.

What are OBEs?

OBEs are reported experiences that occur shortly after a person's body has been rendered unconscious by sleep. They were formerly referred to as "astral projections" or "dreams." OBEs are often psychic in nature, involving some form of extrasensory perception (ESP). In other cases they are purely physical, and related to lucid dreaming or false awakenings.

What is out-of-body projection?

Out-of-body projection is a type of astral projection that involves a sensation of seeing the physical world from an area outside one's physical body. It has also been reported that during an OBE, people have been able to hear, smell, taste, feel touch and even move objects with their thoughts. Some reports say that the spirit may leave the body without a sensation of movement, and these are sometimes referred to as flying saucers. Out-of-body projection is often used to refer to both OBEs and OBEs involving flying.

What is reincarnation?

Reincarnation involves the idea that people have lived before in other bodies and that they return in different ones again millennia or even thousands of years later. Reincarnation has been reported by various cultures throughout time, and although it may be linked to folklore, there is no scientific proof it actually occurs. Because there is no evidence for reincarnation, most scientists do not accept this concept as a reality.

What is a psychic attack?

Psychic attacks can occur when one person or another sends harmful thoughts toward the victim. Most people are not aware that they are being targeted in this way. The emotional and physical effects of psychic attacks can vary from person to person. Psychic attacks often lead to other negative side effects such as anxiety, self-doubt, depression, and sleep problems. One example is "vortexing," which induces irritability, nausea, dizziness, fatigue, or exhaustion in the victim. Another type of attack is "entering," which involves an aggressor directly influencing the thoughts or actions of another individual through telepathy (without having established contact). Entities or spirits can also be the source of psychic attacks.

What are demons?

Many people believe that demons are evil spiritual beings who torment humans. These negative forces are often associated with the devil or Satan, but others say that demons can exist independently from the devil. Demons may take possession of individuals and cause them to have hallucinations, suffer from multiple personality disorder, experience unwanted sexual behavior, or commit suicide. Victims are encouraged to seek help by religious professionals such as priests or nuns. They also prescribe exorcisms because they believe the situation is a spiritual one and cannot be resolved through conventional medicine. Exorcisms are not performed by licensed medical professionals.

What is the evil eye?

The evil eye is a term used in some cultures to describe an individual or an object that makes another person look bad, making them seem to be inferior or damaged. The idea of the evil eye originated from ancient superstitions that said that people who looked at another person with envy were actually looking at the person's soul, which was then captured in a doll-like object that was hung on their house to bring the negative energies back home. In some other cultures, the evil eye is believed to be a supernatural force and can be caused by either magical or natural means. It is believed to cause harm or death to the victim it has been cast upon.

Ghosts are believed to be the spirits of dead people that appear in our world; they are often associated with paranormal activity. People have described seeing ghosts that resemble their loved ones, friends, or even strangers. Some people believe that ghosts are the souls of the dead; others think they are manifestations of energy that cannot break free from this dimension. Ghosts can appear as solid, translucent, or ethereal beings and can either disappear or remain visible for some time after they are first seen.

What is a poltergeist?

Poltergeists are believed to be the spirits of dead people who appear in our world. Unlike ghosts, they are thought to manifest themselves through disturbing physical activity that causes damage or defacement. They can manifest themselves as translucent, solid, or ethereal beings and can either disappear or remain visible for some time after their first appearance. Some poltergeist cases have been associated with cases involving demonic possession.

What is a haunting?

Haunting is a phenomenon that involves the experience of paranormal activity such as spontaneous paranormal perceptual phenomena and unexplained sounds such as strange noises, voices, or footsteps from unseen persons or objects. Some people believe that ghosts are the cause of haunting, but research has not shown any connection between these two phenomena.

What is the Enfield haunting?

The Enfield Haunting was a poltergeist incident that occurred in the early 1970s in Enfield, England. It involved four people: Margaret Hodgson (the "primary witness"), her twelve-year-old daughter Janet (the "secondary witness"), and eleven-year-old nephew Johnny.

One night at approximately 3 a.m., Janet and Johnny awoke to discover that their beds had been knocked over, some of their clothing was missing, and the house was on fire. In ten days there were similar events, including damaged furniture and possessions moving on their own. It is believed that this incident is not a poltergeist case because the children were able to interact with the spirit and were able to influence it without being harmed or taken advantage of.

Astral projection is the process by which people leave their physical bodies while they are still alive. It has been observed in various cultures throughout world history, but it does not have scientific proof that it occurs.

Astral projection is thought to be caused by believe in reincarnation or previous lifetimes. It involves a person leaving their body to travel outside of the physical world but still being able to communicate with the living. In this way people can leave their bodies and travel through other dimensions.

What is mind reading?

Mind reading is purported to occur when one person can know what another person is thinking without having physical contact. The majority of individuals believe that the ability to read thoughts or intentions does not happen often, but there have been documented cases where mind readers have provided accurate information about people's pasts, present decisions, and future intentions. These are known as "telepathic" abilities and appear most frequently in children.

What is hauntology?

Hauntology refers to the study of the paranormal, malicious or occult activities, and poltergeists. It is used to categorize haunted locations either as being "haunted" or "lost". It has been suggested that places that have had strange or unexplained activity should be studied to learn from them and prevent the occurrence of similar events in the future. It is described as a field with potential for advancing understanding and knowledge of poltergeists.

What are sleep paralysis?

Sleep paralysis is an uncommon occurrence where one experiences muscle paralysis during REM (rapid eye movement) sleep. These episodes are also referred to as "night terrors". They occur when you wake up in the middle of the night and are unable to move because your body is asleep. You may be able to hear and feel what is happening in your sleep, but you cannot wake up from this state.

What is lucid dreaming?

Lucid dreaming is a phenomenon where a person can dream while being aware that they are dreaming. This state allows for control of the dream environment as well as action within it and awareness of the situation. Being able to control your dreams allows for creative experiences about what you wish would happen in your life or for ways to solve problems you may be having that seem unsolvable during waking life.

What is a past life regression?

Past life regression is a phenomenon where an individual can experience the memories of previous lifetimes. This phenomenon has not been accepted by the scientific community, but it could be induced by hypnosis or other means that induce trance-like states. Some people believe that past life regression can prove that reincarnation exists.

What is a faith healing?

Faith healing is a practice that involves the healing of physical ailments by laying on hands or through prayer. The practice has been used by many cultures throughout history and was used to prove the power of their gods. It continues to be used in religious practices and this practice has been observed throughout world history for thousands of years.

What is channeling?

Channeling is the practice of contacting a spirit or entity and relaying its messages to another person. These messages can be personal, mundane, or paranormal in nature, but they are believed to come from a spiritual being outside of the channeler's normal perception abilities. Channeling has been practiced by many individuals who have claimed to be able to contact dead spirits and other beings and share with others what they hear. This ability is thought to be bestowed upon them by higher powers such as angels.

What are astral projection experiences?

Astral projection experiences tend to occur during sleep or in a trance-like state due to the effects of meditation or drug use. In this state the individual leaves the physical body and in a way may be able to experience events that occur in other dimensions. These experiences tend to be more terrifying due to the lack of control and knowledge that you can have.

What is automatic writing?

Automatic writing is a practice where someone who claims to have direct access to non-human entities such as spirits, angels, demons, or gods writes words or sentences without being aware of what he/she is doing. The messages might come through messages from the spirit but they can also be mundane sentences that are merely coming through by association. Automatic writings are used as evidence against pseudoscience and occult practices such as astral projection.

What is a spirit box?

A spirit box is a device that creates white noise and allows people to ask questions or say prayers. The spirit box might receive answers in the form of crackling noises. The device has been used to test paranormal activity and can also be used as entertainment. The machine has not been proven to be effective at finding spirits or demons, but some believe it is worth a try and fun for those who like ghost hunting.

What are the poltergeist phenomena?

The poltergeist phenomena are a series of paranormal events that occur without warning and occur around an individual. The key characteristics of these phenomena are that they occur around specific individuals and often involve noise, movement of objects, and the incidence of fires. These events have been documented as early as the 1700s with Jakob Friedrich Friesen. Friesen is known for making reports on poltergeist cases that occurred around his servant and himself.

What are levitation phenomena?

Levitation phenomena occur when an individual seems to float in the air with no support or outside power source. This phenomenon can be associated to many paranormal locations including haunted houses and historical locations that are said to be haunted. They have been documented as early as the 1600s. Many individuals claim to be able to float objects in the air and this can be done through various means such as mental concentration.

What is an evil eye?

The "evil eye" is a common superstition where one has the belief that the eyes or attention of others can bring harm, misfortune, or negativity. The term "evil eye" comes from the ideas of a person who has the ability to do harm to another through their eyes alone. In many cultures, it has been held as fact that someone with this ability can cause tragedy and death to others just by looking at them. There are many stories of individuals who have been saved from evil by wearing an amulet or other method against receiving the eye's malady.

What are the paranormal events of the night?

The paranormal events of the night refer to a series of paranormal experiences that occur at night. The experiences and experiences are often perceived as frightening or bizarre. These occurrences can take place within houses, graveyards, abandoned structures, and in other places that are thought to be haunted. The phenomenon often occurs due to an increase in negative energy that is present at night as people sleep or during the day when people aren't outside for long periods of time.

A haunting is an unexplained event where one feels they are being watched or followed by a ghost (or ghosts). They may also feel like their whole body is being invaded by something unseen. These events can occur at home and in other areas. There is a belief that these haunting are communications from the dead in order to relay a message to the living. Haunting happen at night and many believe them to be due to paranormal activities such as spirits or demons. Many believe they are caused by negative energy and certain events, like deaths or murders, which increase the possibility of the perpetration of paranormal activity.

What is shadow people?

Shadow people refers to unexplained sightings of black figures that seem to play tricks on people or scare them. These black figures have been described as looking like a silhouette of a man with arms extended out in front of him and his head cocked back facing upwards. The figure is black and not transparent. This sighting can occur during times when there doesn't seem to be anyone around. Shadow people are not thought to be dangerous to the individual who sees them, but instead they are a sign that a paranormal experience may be occurring in your area.

What is an alien abduction?

An alien abduction is the idea that an person has experienced being taken away against his/her will by alien beings from another planet in order to study or experiment on them. This has also sometimes been referred to as "missing time experiences." The term was coined by UFO researcher Budd Hopkins who studied abductee stories and found many common characteristics including those of missing time and bathing suit areas of skin. The idea of abductions has been met with skepticism and scientists have determined there is no physiological evidence that these events are taking place.

What are vampires?

A vampire is a mythical being that lives off the blood of other living creatures. This creature originated in stories from Eastern Europe and was brought over to the United States by immigrants. Vampires were originally perceived as evil beings but they have become more popularized as romantic figures in pop culture. The myth of vampirism seems to stem from people underlying fear of death and the unknown, which can be traced back to ancient times when disease such as rabies and tuberculosis were not understood.

What is a ghost?

A ghost is a supernatural being that seems to haunt the living. Many ghosts are thought to be spirits of people who have died. The idea of ghosts has been around since the beginning of time and reflects human thoughts on death. Many believe a person can become a ghost after their death in which they are not able to rest in peace and remain with their loved ones.

What are astral projections?

Astral projection is the idea that one can leave his/her body or the physical world and travel into an alternate parallel dimension outside of our known universe where all matter is composed of energy and cannot be detected by our senses. This phenomenon can occur while awake or during sleep, but remains difficult to trace down. It is said to be a very natural phenomenon that happens in our minds.

What is sleep paralysis?

Sleep paralysis is an experience of waking up during the night and being unable to move or speak. This can last from a few seconds to several minutes and it usually happens when a person first wakes up. It can also happen if you are woken up suddenly from your sleep or during REM cycles. The experiences may seem real but they have been found to be hallucinations by doctors who research the area. These happenings are often thought of as scary but are not dangerous in any way.

Is religion a factor of paranormal activity?

Religion is often thought of in terms of how it affects human behavior, society and everyday life. However, religion can also be known for being a supernatural force in which it can influence objects or people to behave in certain ways. The idea of something being out of the ordinary due to something supernatural happening is referred to as paranormal activity. For example, returning from the dead and communicating with the living is considered an act that has been attributed to religious beliefs.

What are poltergeists?

What is human-animal hybrids?

Human-animal hybrids seem to be a type of paranormal creature that appears in the form of a half-human, half-animal creature. These creatures tend to stand on two legs and have a more ape like appearance than other animals. They have also been known as werewolves, shapeshifters or various other names depending on their appearance. These creatures are usually seen in people's dreams or hallucinations and have been popularized in literature such as Dr. Jekyll and Mr. Hyde.

What is aliens?

Aliens are creatures from another planet who may either be physical beings or in the form of energy. They have been a common theme throughout many cultures since ancient times. The idea of an alien species communicating with humans has become celebrated in pop culture such as television shows, movies and even video games. The ideas of these creatures vary from advanced beings with technology to those that remain primitive.

What is obsession?

Obsession is a nagging feeling you get that tells you to engage in an activity more frequently than others do. It is a fixation with something that you wish to do or have become associated with. This is one of the most common forms of paranormal activity and can be a symptom of schizophrenia or other mental disorders.

How do ghosts appear?

Many ghosts seem to appear as orbs, mist, figures, spots on the wall or movement in the corner of your eye when you are looking elsewhere. These types of experiences tend to happen when people are alone in an area for a long period of time. It may become a regular occurrence for some people and make them feel uneasy if they see it too much. The idea that ghosts are spirits from another world has encouraged people to believe they are being followed at night or something is watching them from afar.

People who believe in poltergeists claim that there are moving objects that have no source but show up from time to time in homes and other places. Items such as dishes or furniture can be broken and picked up by something unseen. It has been found that many people who believe in poltergeists are more likely to participate in paranormal activities than those who do not believe. There has been no real evidence found that proves poltergeist activity to be real, but many people continue to claim they have experiences.

IS ASTRAL PROJECTING DANGEROUS?

Astral projection is a technique for the out of body experience. It's been practiced for centuries and can be used to cultivate a strong sense of spirituality.

But it's not without its dangers. There are documented cases people who have died, or gone insane after practicing astral projection. And, because you are in such a vulnerable state when you're out of your body, it's quite easy for other people to take advantage of you.

At the same time, there are those who claim that astral projection is a safe, beneficial experience.

So what's the truth? Is astral projection safe or dangerous? I'll tell you right now. The answer depends on who you are. It depends on how spiritual you already are, because astral projection can lead to even more spiritual development. It can lead to a heightened awareness and understanding of what is going on around you, which is especially useful if you live in an area where people are not very spiritual or open minded about spirituality at all.

So, I think the best way to answer the question, "Is astral projection dangerous?" is with another question:

"How spiritual are you when you start practicing astral projection?" The answer is: It depends.

It depends on many things. It depends on how spiritual you already are.

If you feel that you are only going to be using astral projection to have fun, then it entirely depends on what I call the "trivialization of the spiritual." If you think that astral projection is just something fun and interesting that people do to enhance their spirituality, then yes. It's perfectly safe.

But if you see it as an opportunity for spiritual growth – really, truly seeing yourself as part of a vast network of interconnected souls – then chances are very good that your mental health will take a real beating. The experience will be full of overwhelming emotions like doubt, depression and sadness.

You may get so lost in the experience that you end up feeling like a lost and depressed child, or you may have some crazy experiences that make you feel like insane.

It could change your life forever.

The truth is that astral projection is something everyone should be doing. Everyone should be experiencing it at least once during their lifetime. And everyone can benefit from astral projection in some way, whether they are experiencing it right now or not.

There are many different theories about astral projection. People who have experienced it firsthand say that they feel like they are being pulled out of their body, and then they find themselves floating around in the air or floating outside of their bedroom window, or somewhere else entirely.

But scientists say this has no basis in reality at all. They say that the feeling of being pulled out is just a result of the brain and body shutting down as you fall asleep, and then your "astral body" is mistakenly interpreted by your consciousness as if it were a separate entity entirely from yourself.

But in the end, does any of this really matter? Does it matter whether astral projection is real or not? Does it matter if you "come back" from astral projection at all or if you are just imagining things?

I'd say that none of these things matter at all. They don't matter because they both result in the same thing: a heightened understanding of reality. As long as you can experience what I call "the out of body experience," then you can reap most of the benefits that come with experiencing yourself as an entity separate from your body.

Just like everyone benefits from walking, everyone benefits from doing astral projection. It's natural and good for us to want to step out of our physical shell and see the world in a different way. We want something more than what we get from this life, that's true. We're searching for something more.

But what if you're not yet ready to "step out" of your body? What if you're still not sure that you should "step out?" Many people start practicing astral projection as an easy and enjoyable way to have fun, but that's actually the worst way to do it.

Most people learn astral projection as a way to have fun without learning the difficult part. They start out by falling asleep during the day and then they imagine themselves being pulled out of their body, floating around in space or whatever.

But when you do astral projection correctly, it's not about imagining things at all. It's about relying on yourself to really experience your own inner reality. It's about having enough self-control and discipline to make the experience truly yours, no matter how difficult that may be.

It's very important that you start with a sense of mindfulness and commitment to your practice. That's the reason I created the "Stepping out Course." I want you to take this seriously and to understand that if you do astral projection, it will be hard work. It could even be a struggle at times. And you may have some painful moments or feelings – it could make you feel overwhelmed and beyond depressed.

It's important to understand that these things are part of the process as you step out of your body. But if you get caught up in them, then they'll prevent you from achieving your goal, which is learning about yourself as a soul while experiencing reality in a different way than before.

Over the next few weeks and months, I'm going to guide you through everything from finding an experience of your own, to learning how to enter a state of light where your awareness is so deep that it's nearly impossible for you to feel anything at all.

Through my teachings on The Stepping out Course, I will help you put everything together from your spiritual practice into a cohesive whole.

This is the first time that you've learned how to listen to yourself when you're doing astral projection, and it's also the first time that you've made a decision of your own about what kind of life you want, even when it feels like nobody wants you. And this is something that everybody needs.

So it's important for me to tell you that this will not be easy. It could be a struggle. And if you're not ready to face reality, then this isn't for you. You should stay where you are in your life and don't even think about this right now.

But if you are ready to face your destiny, and if you're ready to understand yourself as a soul who has had many lifetimes, and who will have more lifetimes in the future, then this is the course for you.

I am going to walk you through everything, step by step. I'm going to teach you how to enter the light, and then how to actually experience yourself as your soul. Then we will turn your awareness inward and learn how to know who you are within yourself. And then finally, we will look outward with your soul's eyes and see what's there in the world outside of yourself.

I want you to understand that this is not a magic trick where you can be pulled out of your body and see "the other side." This is something that happens inside of us, but it happens within a very deep state of reality where nothing else exists except for our own inner awareness.

As you practice astral projection, you will find that everything in the world begins to make sense. You will see why things are the way they are, and you will begin to see the truth of things. This is good, because if you don't understand why things are the way they are, then you won't be able to make sense of them. And if you can't make sense of something, then how can you change it?

To understand yourself as a soul is to understand your connection with reality itself. This training will help you become more aware of how your thoughts change your reality, and it will help you learn how to think in ways that lead to your own spiritual rebirth and enlightenment.

I want you to know that this is the most important thing you will ever do. I can't tell you if it's going to be painful or difficult, but if you decide to learn astral projection, then it will be.

If you want a bit of fun, then by all means go out and do some astral projection every night! But even then, what are you really doing? If your goals are anything other than spiritual awakening and enlightenment, then this is not the right path for you.

But if your goal is really to learn about yourself as a soul while experiencing reality in a different way than before, then I guarantee that anything I teach in my course will help with that. And I've been doing this work for many years, and I can guarantee that if you do the practice in my Stepping Out Course, then you will achieve your goal.

You will learn astral projection by doing it every day for several weeks. Then you will enter the light and see yourself as a soul while experiencing reality in a way that's impossible to experience before.

And along the way, I will teach you everything from how to get started with your spiritual practice to how to make changes in your life so that they lead toward enlightenment instead of away from it. This is where all of the real learning is going to take place.

So if you're ready, then I look forward to teaching you about yourself as a soul. Then you'll understand why people come into your life, why they go away, and how they can be useful to you if you let them. And how to focus on your own spiritual development by moving beyond yourself.

ESSENTIAL ENERGY CONCEPTS

What is an astral body?

- How can we access the astral plane?

- What happens in an out of body experience?

Astral projection, or astral travel, can be defined as the act of consciously leaving one's physical body and exploring the (higher) planes. It is called "astral" because it uses a different type of matter than that which composes our physical bodies. The use of this different matter allows our otherwise limited human brains to explore places otherwise not accessible to us.

It is important to note that the lights (physical bodies) of other people and animals are not projected. We are able to see them because they are not separated (as we are) from their physical body. When we leave our physical bodies, we become what is called a "projected being", that is, an object which can be clearly perceived by external beings (such as other human beings and possibly animals).

A common misconception regarding Astral Projection is the belief that one can project themselves outside of their own body. This is not true. While one can move his/her eyes and hands and head temporarily outside of his or her body, the physical body cannot be projected outside of feet, hands etc.

A popular example of when Astral Projection occurs is the common experience of seeing something "out of the corner of one's eye". This is not possible unless one is not in their physical body. Otherwise, a physical brain would cause the eyes to move in order to see. This movement, called "visual agnosia" (or visual amnesia), is impossible without a physical body.

In addition, most people who are experienced with Astral Projection have experienced sensations of floating outside their own body for at least a few minutes. The experiences can also vary from person to person ("astral nausea") or even be unnoticeable ("floating above myself"). When people are not really experienced with Astral Projection it is often very hard to notice and distinguish between one's physical body and other objects around them.

A common belief is that, like the physical world we inhabit, the astral plane is composed of matter as opposed to energy. This is a logical assumption as both the physical plane and the astral plane are made up of various combinations of atoms and molecules (such as water).

Astral projection in our normal state of consciousness:

In our normal state of consciousness, most people cannot project themselves. This occurs because when we become conscious, we can only think about things that we have experienced before in our lives. Most people have never experienced being "out of their bodies" therefore it is not something they can think about consciously.

Through practice and training, it is possible for anyone to learn how to project themselves. This practice/training (called "soul work") involves a person's soul travelling outside of their physical body in a natural way (i.e. without any form of external interference from another source). When this happens, there may be no incense burning or candles lit and there may not even be any special higher states of consciousness reached at all. The only difference when the person returns to their physical body is that they feel "energized".

While this is the final stage of an actual astral projection session, it is not necessary to experience this stage before others. For example, someone may be able to protect themselves from their physical body without experiencing a full out astral projection at all.

Why do people experience "astral nausea"?

"Astral nausea", also called "astral inertia", is a sensation that people have when they first start attempting an astral projection. It is described as an uncomfortable feeling of heaviness or fullness in the head, neck, and chest area. The sensation can also be experienced in other body parts: for example, tingling sensations (including numbness) and sudden muscle twitching can occur. These sensations usually continue until the astral projection.

These sensations are caused by the physical body trying to prevent the soul from leaving it. The soul, of course, is not heavy and cannot cause this sensation. It is accurate to say that because of their negative attitudes, some non-astral projectors will experience an uncomfortable sensation within their physical bodies before they can properly project themselves out of their bodies. This is not required and does not mean that they will fail the attempt at astral projection.

"Astral nausea" is also sometimes seen in someone who struggles with being grounded (i.e., connected with their physical body) while they are projecting themselves out of it. During this type of astral projection, a person can find themselves hanging in the air. This is a natural phase of an astral projection (called "floating"), and is not dangerous. One should know that simply by willing themselves to float on their backs, they will slowly drift downwards until they are at a normal height again.

A fact that most people don't know is that if we meditate for long enough while in a higher state of consciousness (such as theta), it may eventually reach the point where our soul separates from our physical body. This is similar to a coma patient who has entered a deep sleep state.

The reason why most people do not succeed at astral projection is because they are not ready for it. They have never developed the proper mental and physical conditions necessary for being able to do it. Therefore, they must return to their physical body right before the projection or else they may return in such a state of consciousness that their mind cannot handle it and they might end up hitting their head on something (resulting in damage).

The real difference between a successful astral projection attempt and any mental high is that when you are already in your body, whether one succeeds or not, there will be certain physical sensations that accompany it. For example, people often experience a "rush" of energy when they begin the projection. This is often described as a feeling of the body increasing in size.

This is not a high or an induced state of consciousness, but rather just the physical body beginning to react to its projected environment (which is now very different than what it experienced while physically present). Because these sensations can be quite intense, one should be careful that they do not become too great and damage their physical body. While this is rare with more experienced projector's, beginners should avoid overdoing it. If you feel pain during this process you are probably doing too much; relax and wait until it diminishes before continuing the projection again.

The main reason why most people do not succeed at astral projection is because they are not willing to perform the necessary mental exercises needed for the practice. Some of these exercises include:

Hannah Stouffer, a famous mystic who was very successful in her astral projections as well as her physical lives, wrote an article in which she gave good advice on how to succeed at projecting oneself.

Also, there is a book that is very helpful in teaching people how to succeed at astral projection. This book is called "How to Project Your Astral Body" and can be found here. This book should be read by anyone attempting to project their astral bodies, including all non-astral projectors.

Finally, although it should be obvious, a huge factor in most people's failure at astral projection is the way they are thinking about it. They are either thinking too much about what they can do (i.e., "I'm going to have a great time flying around the world!") or else they are not thinking enough about what they need to do (i.e. "I need to relax.") These people will not be able to make their astral projection attempts very successful.

It is better to do nothing than only half-do something. If you want to have a good astral projection experience, your goals should be the following:

The general mindset one should have during an astral projection is that they are doing something that can change their lives for the better. The person should look at this as an opportunity for them to enjoy themselves and to have a good time. They should also know that there is no pressure on them, and if they do it right, they will have a good experience.

To successfully astral project your first attempt should be a positive experience. It is best not to try and force yourself unless you are experienced in being able to successfully astral project on your first attempt (which most beginners will not be.). Instead you should relax, and if you are capable of doing it on your first try, then you will be able to do it. If not, don't worry about it; at least you tried it.

After that most important mindset has been achieved, the next step is to make your attempts at astral projection easier using the techniques outlined in the next lesson.

Astral Projection in a Nutshell: A Quick Summary

To achieve and maintain an astral projection from start to finish one must perform the following steps:

1. Meditate and enter deep alpha state. You can use either a body relaxation technique or else a mantra meditation. The mantra meditation, if properly done, will take you to the beginning of theta. After this you are ready to do a projection attempt.

2. Use an OBE technique to project yourself out of your body. A good way to achieve this is by imagining that you are getting pulled out of your body by someone else (or else that your astral body is being scooped up by an invisible force outside of yourself).

3. Once you are outside of your physical body, look for the astral door in front of you and go through it. You should now be in the astral plane.

4. Stay there for a few hours, or else you can instantly return to your physical body by mentally commanding it to happen.

5. If you wish to remain astral traveling for a longer period of time, then simply use the techniques explained in the next lesson on lucid dreaming (lucid dreaming is when your mind has 'awakened') to make this happen.

6. After the experience, reenter your physical body and rest until awake or else command yourself back into the astral plane. And that is the end of your first astral projection.

Completing Your First Astral Projection Successfully

You should try and have a successful astral projection that will be memorable for the rest of your life. For this reason, and because you should really want it to happen, you should give it your best shot. This is the time for you to practice hard and accept nothing less than success. If you do this while being mindful of what you are doing, then there is no reason why you cannot enjoy yourself in any way possible if you wish to do so.

After your first successful astral projection, you should feel better about yourself. You have experienced something that few people, if any at all, have had the good luck to experience in their lives. And this feeling of accomplishment is worth keeping with you for a long time, especially if you realize how hard it was to accomplish this your first time around.

Why do most people fail at astral projection? Because they are not willing to make themselves fully comfortable and relaxed enough during their projections. Sometimes they try to use OBE techniques which are awkward and difficult to perform successfully under pressure; sometimes they try and use OBE techniques when they are too tired to be able perform them properly; or sometime they try but simply cannot accomplish it.

Astral projection is a somewhat difficult project to accomplish, but with enough dedication and practice, anyone can astral project. It is all about making yourself feel comfortable enough to let your mind do what it needs to do in order to get the job done.

Once you are able to have a successful first astral projection you will be able to continue having successful ones for the rest of your life. The only thing that you will need to do differently for each one is read up on any new techniques that might be available (for example, if you have given up on a certain technique before then now might be the time for you to try it again).

In short, a successful first astral projection should give you a good reason to continue practicing the art of astral projection.

BASICS OF ASTRAL PROJECTION

Astral projection is a method of "traveling" outside your body. Astral projection can be done in many ways and as an astral projector, you will find that it is easy to adjust to other dimensions. The key to learning this technique is curiosity and practice.

Here are some astral projection basics to help you get started. There are many books on this topic that can help you.

Astral projection is an excellent way for expanding one's consciousness and understanding their true nature as spirit.

The first thing you need to understand is your basic energy body. It is projection of your energy body, but it is also called astral projection because your consciousness moves outside your physical body during the process. There are different ways to project your energy body outside of its physical shell and we will explore some methods below. However, before we begin exploring all these cool ways to project, let's take a look at what you will be projecting from and into and how all this works in terms of the human body.

Think of your energy body as a layer you wear over your physical body. It is invisible to the naked eye, but is attached to you through a tube or cord which originates from the center of your chest. A lot of people call this cord or tube a silver cord or something similar. At the end of this cord there are energy 'hands' which can be used to manipulate objects around you, which we will discuss later. When you are not projecting, this silver tube should be invisible unless there are astral leaks that prevent it from remaining unseen.

To regain your consciousness, you will use an abrupt action that will dislodge the silver cord. This is easy to do and there are several ways to do it with different results depending on the situation. A better way is to have a friend or family member help you by doing it for you when you are sleeping.

After gaining your consciousness, there are different things you could be seeing around you depending on your own personal experiences or what has been shown to others in books and what not.

There are several ways of projecting your consciousness outside of your body, and I will provide descriptions in the order that best start to explain some of the methods. There are those who believe that only the extreme case of astral projection is actually seeing the astral plane or planes themselves. This is incorrect as there are many different ways and they all work together to allow you access to these higher realms.

The first method would be known as Projective Identification. You become aware of your energy body and its location. At this point, you could be seeing the astral plane, but not necessarily. Your consciousness is still trapped in a human body on earth and you are simply beginning to explore this new realm.

To describe Projective Identification, think of it as the ability to project yourself outside your body into the astral dimension. This is a very simple form of astral projection that basically requires a willing or open mind and energy awareness.

This is the most basic form of astral projection and the most common way to learn it. It is called Projective Identification because you project your consciousness outward so that you can identify and recognize this astral plane. There are many tricks and things that can go wrong with this technique, so please be careful not to use it as an accident.

There are different versions of Projective Identification, but this is one that I have used many times with success. You need to focus on your energy body and visualize it clearly. In other words, you are practicing energy awareness at this point so that you can become aware of your energy body and all its parts as well as the details of the surrounding area where it resides (the physical body).

Another way that this can be described is when you look in a mirror and see the refection of yourself. The mirror image is actually a reflection of your 'energy body' and as you know, there isn't really a physical body in that reflection because it is all made up of light/energy particles reflecting off the mirror. The same goes for what you will see when projecting yourself outside your body. The only difference is that when you are projecting, you will see your energy body with the surrounding environment. You will be able to differentiate it from the surroundings because it is in a different location and has some depth to it.

Once you have practiced this technique and felt confident in your ability to see the energy body, then you can move on to more advanced techniques or just stick with this one because it is a very simple one to learn and master.

Another method is known as Astral Tribulation or Observation. You basically watch yourself as if from a distance outside of yourself and observe what happens as you do various actions or things. In other words, you are seeing your own energy body from a distance and observing what happens as you move certain parts of your energy body or manipulate things around you. This is rather simple in concept but can be hard to master because it takes some effort to achieve this level of awareness. This is why I don't really suggest doing this on purpose before going to sleep unless you are really dedicated or have no choice in the matter. It has worked for me several times over the years though, and I find that it is a good way to practice without falling asleep at the same time.

This has some similarities to Projective Identification, but it is different in that you are seeing your energy body from a distance, not just identifying it. Also, you can see parts of your energy body or things around you, so the effect is similar to what Projective Identification will be like once you gain more experience and become more aware of your energy body.

Another useful technique is called Astral Travel. This requires that you have a clear intention while asleep. At first, all you will be able to do is move at an extremely slow rate while still remaining conscious. As time passes, this increases until eventually very fast movement levels out and becomes normal for you.

This is a very popular phenomenon that people do on purpose. It is, however, only helpful if you are trying to reach a higher plane of existence and are not simply experimenting with it. Astral Travel can also occur automatically or spontaneously while dreaming at night or just before waking up in the morning. In these cases, you will be taken to a certain destination and may be brought back after having an 'experience'. This depends on your own personal experiences as well as the effects of your astral body interacting with the physical one while you live your life during the day time. Again, this technique requires that you have a clear intention while asleep and that you are fully aware while doing it.

Astral Projection can be used when you want to leave your physical body after having a dream and wake up with everything just as you left it. You will be able to move around like an astral being, but you will still be fully conscious and awake in your physical body.

There are many different types of astral projection and the one that I am describing here is the simplest one, the one that is most popular among beginners. It is also the easiest to learn as well. In fact, I used this type of astral projection myself for a while until I discovered that some of the other techniques were more powerful and better suited for my personal needs as an advanced student of astral projection.

Astral Projection can be done by anyone as long as they have the desire to do it. As I mentioned before, there are many different types of astral projection and what I am describing here is a basic form that nearly everyone will be able to do, no matter what their skill level is when it comes to things like meditation and energy manipulation. It also requires an understanding of the energy body and how to see it while remaining conscious.

There are two popular methods of doing this; you can either do it by leaving your physical body behind or you can leave the astral projection body behind and take your physical one with you. In other words, you are moving between two bodies at different locations.

This is a very helpful technique because it requires less effort to learn than some of the others. It also doesn't require that much energy output, in fact, most people find that they have more energy after doing this than when they started out. This is because they are able to move around while being in an unconscious state, therefore regulating their energy much better than they would have if they had stayed in their physical bodies.

Some people who practice this often are able to move around a lot faster and with more ease than others. This is because all of their attention has been focused on the astral body and it has become more solid as well as stronger over time through use. It is important to understand though that you won't be able to do this right away, it takes practice just like any other type of projection or energy manipulation.

This kind of astral projection can also appear like a lucid dream where you have full control over what happens and what you see. You will still be dreaming, but you will have full control over it as if you were awake. This form of astral projection is the same as just waking up from a dream and moving around, except with this technique you can stay conscious and not wake up. You can also move at nearly any speed that you want, much faster than during sleep, if your energy body is strong enough to support that.

There are also many different techniques to use during astral projection that give the appearance of being conscious while there are actually no thoughts going through your mind whatsoever. These can include things like imagination, imagery or visualization. These techniques are fun and useful in their own right, they can be used to induce astral projection or lucid dreaming.

The simple version that I mentioned before is the easiest and most well known technique. It works very well if you have a clear intention and want to use your astral body while remaining conscious. It is also possible to use this for out of body experiences where you are simply sitting in your house or somewhere else doing nothing and then your physical body just falls asleep.

This is a little more difficult to learn than the first technique, but not by much, especially if you already know how to meditate properly. After you have learned it, you will be able to immediately do this and see a little more clearly the difference between what is actually happening and your thoughts about it.

There are many other advanced techniques that you can learn as well, but this one is usually enough to get people started. It is also a very good starting point for anyone who wants to learn astral projection, as it is simple and easy to understand. You can also control what happens during an out of body experience in this way, so you can even try exploring different dimensions if your interest prompts you to do so. All of these techniques also work for astral traveling as well, but they are more difficult than any of the ones I have mentioned here.

It is a good idea to learn about astral projection in advance because it is something that you can use to explore all of the other dimensions that we live here on earth. It isn't hard to do it, but it is important to know how and why you are doing it if you want to be fully conscious while doing it. You also need an understanding of the differences between your physical body and your astral body in order for this kind of movement between the two while remaining conscious.

Once you have learned how to do this, using your astral body will become extremely easy and natural while being conscious at all times. There are many different types of out of body experiences as well as options for how they can happen. They range from exploring a different dimension where you can travel anywhere in it, to traveling somewhere that has already been explored by other people before and trying to remember what happened.

Also, if your intention is to explore the other dimensions while being conscious and not accidentally getting stuck in one of them or lost in the void between them, you need much more experience with the different energy body techniques. I will talk about that later on when I introduce you to some of the advanced techniques.

Physical Projection: The unconscious movement away from physical reality

The most popular form of astral projection is actually moving away from the physical world completely, even while still being conscious. This kind of project is more powerful than the normal type you have been reading about, but it also requires a lot more energy to use. It can start as an accidental move or even be triggered by some kind of trauma.

This kind of projection may also require more attention than most people can give it, especially if you are moving with those around you. It is important to know that this type of movement can be used in both directions from the physical world and in other dimensions as well. You can leave your physical body and go back into it, as well as travel completely away from it.

Out of body experiences in the physical world can happen for a variety of reasons. The easiest way that most people experience this is simply falling asleep, while in their physical body, and then waking up immediately after that with no recollection at all about what happened.

You could also be in a situation where there is some kind of trauma, especially one that scares you a lot, and the next thing you know you are out of your body and floating around somewhere else. Many people find themselves hanging around their homes after they have had such an experience because they have been scared by whatever they saw or experienced during their projection.

ASTRAL BODY

Astral body projection is a power associated with the astral body and is defined as the phenomenon of an astral body that leaves the physical body to travel in various levels of dream and reality. Some use it to explore past lives, or just their imagination. This power has been used for centuries by mystics, spiritual leaders, monks, nuns and ascetics. They visit higher spirit realms in search for knowledge and truth. Some use it to heal themselves and others.

Those who possess this power may not be aware of it. In many cases, the first indication was recollection of a past life experience. Many will say that they felt possessed by a spirit, or that they were channeling information from someone else. It seems obvious after they have gone through the whole process that they actually had projected their astral body and were able to travel outside their body to visit other places in the universe.

The most astounding part about projection is the fact that we all have this capability but are not aware of it because we do not remember having done so. We could have done it in a past life, or we could have learned the skill from someone else. There are also many books that teach you how to do this skill.

Some people believe they can leave their bodies without falling unconscious after death, which is a misconception.

Leaving the physical body does not mean consciousness doesn't leave your body, but rather you still retain consciousness while leaving the physical body as long as you keep breathing, because air still makes its way into the lungs. The moment you stop breathing, consciousness leaves the physical body for good.

Some people may have done this on their own and not realized it. The first indication is usually recollection of a past life experience. The next indication may be a presence in your room...one that you can feel but cannot see. In some cases, they can touch you, but you cannot touch them. You may hear them talking around you, and not realize that they are actually talking to you. It seems obvious after they have left that the spirit was projecting its astral body and was able to travel outside their body to visit other places in the universe.

To become conscious outside the physical body has always been possible through various techniques used by masters throughout history. It is very difficult to become conscious outside the physical body but many have done it. It requires a tremendous amount of energy, and it is not a common power found in people. They may be aware of the time when they were conscious in another dimension without knowing how they achieved it.

You may feel like you are being watched by something, suddenly feel pulled somewhere, or pushed away while opening your eyes. Another sign that you are experiencing astral projection is when you feel numb in your hands or legs after leaving your body.

The moment you fall asleep the body becomes paralyzed in order to prevent you from moving around and injuring yourself physically. Your muscles are relaxed in order to prevent involuntary movement while dreaming. The brain stem will not allow you to do anything that would cause physical injury because it is all automatic, and happens with or without your awareness.

When you try to wake yourself up from a dream by trying to open your eyes, you are only able to do so after the brain stem has awakened from the dream state and signals for the eyes to open. While you are dreaming, your eyes are not able to open even if you want them to. You do not have that level of control when dreaming, because your body is paralyzed. The brain stem will not allow you to do anything that would cause physical injury.

In deep sleep we are unable to move our bodies, but that is the point of sleeping in the first place. When fully asleep, your astral body can exit the physical body at will to explore other areas of the universe without any trouble whatsoever. You will experience complete consciousness while in your astral body but still be able to interact with the physical world as to make it appear as if you are still in your physical body.

Your astral body is made of etheric energy and is lighter than your physical body, thus the exit will not create any shock to the system. Due to its light weight, there is no initial impact when separating from the physical body within the three dimensions of time and space. Astral projection can also happen during sleep paralysis (see below), which is why it feels so real. As explained above, hearing voices while experiencing sleep paralysis does not mean you are possessed by a demon or ghost, because it happens before you are fully asleep.

It is possible to have lucid dreams while your astral body is inside your physical body. This means that you are aware that you are dreaming and can consciously interact with the dream world. It requires a lot of practice to learn how to become lucid in this way, but once mastered it is easy to continue. In a dream, your astral body can enter and exit your physical body at will by simply willing it to do so. Often we feel sleep paralysis because we are trying too hard to force our astral body out of our physical body through special breathing exercises, because they do not work effectively. Those techniques only work while asleep.

Astral projection is a process that has a lot of complications around it due to the mainstream belief that it can cause chaos with the physical body and that it can cause multiple personality disorders. Some people want to believe that it is possible, so they do, without ever experiencing it first hand. There is fear of something like this actually happening and the consequences being unknown to them. It seems more realistic if they just cannot believe in something they can't prove its existence physically and scientifically.

It is possible to have lucid dreams while your astral body is inside your physical body. Lucid dreaming is the process of becoming conscious in a dream and being able to interact with the dream world without having to be asleep. It requires uninterrupted concentration as well as lots of practice. Past life memories can be triggered during an astral projection, but they are usually vague and glimpses of past lives only. Tense moments in life may become relived in dreams, but you will not experience the full spectrum of emotions and sensations associated with those moments, only a fraction. To have no control over your thought patterns or actions while dreaming is the result of fear, which causes you to experience fear mixed with frustration.

Astral projection is a step above lucid dreaming. You are aware of your surroundings and you can interact with the physical world. You are also aware that you are dreaming, but your mind is just as active as when you are awake. You can experience an open door to the soul while in a dream and astral projection. Astral projection is a step further than lucid dreaming, because lucid dreams only happen during sleep, and astral projection occurs when physically awake or asleep. During sleep paralysis it feels completely real because your brain has entered the REM state (Rapid Eye Movement) where dreams occur.

In all cases of sleep paralysis, there is no awareness of being conscious in another dimension while outside the physical body at will. Consciousness is still in the physical world, but you are able to separate from your physical body. It feels completely real at the time of the experience, but it is only a dream within a dream of reality. People who experience sleep paralysis may also experience hallucinations while undergoing an astral projection.

ASTRAL PROJECTION TIPS

Astral projection is something that science has brushed aside, but people have known about for a very long time. Here are some tips to help you out!

#1: Keep an open mind. Astral projection is something that goes outside the bounds of conventional science, so it will be hard for scientists and doctors to understand what you're doing if they don't believe in it first.

#2: Keep an open mind about astral projection. Astral projection is something that needs to be done with an open mind, full of curiosity and wonder. Keeping an open mind about it will help you accept what you see as you travel!

#3: Stay positive! If you're negative, astral projection will be hard for you because your body won't let your spirit go because there's no reason for it to do so. That negative state will just drag you down. A positive, happy mindset will be what keeps you from getting lost in the astral!

#4: Don't try to take physical objects with you. You'll just end up losing them, and then it'll be harder to re-find them. And don't try to take any people with you either, because they won't make it back!

#5: Focus on one thing. Get a focus of something that makes sense to you, something that will give your spirit a reason to stay in the body while using astral projection techniques. It can be as simple as concentrating on your next breath or simply focusing on the feeling of being in your body again after leaving it.

#6: Relax. This is a big one! Astral projection is most effective when you are relaxed. If you're stressed out, or anything like that, it'll just pull you back in your body.

"How do I astral project? What are good astral projection techniques?" Astral projection is something that takes practice to do well. The best way to learn how to get out of your body is by practicing, which requires understanding what it does and how it works.

How can I help my children astral project?" Astral projection is something that takes practice to do well.

"How can I help my child stop astral projecting at night? What can a parent do to help their child stop astral projecting?" Astral projection is something that takes practice to do well. The best way to learn how to get out of your body is by practicing, which requires understanding what it does and how it works. But don't worry, there are plenty of ways to go about understanding what exactly astral projection is, and learning how to do it!

IS ASTRAL PROJECTION TRUE?

Paranormal phenomena and entities are characterized as supernatural, and the notion of astral projection is no exception. But what does that mean? What's the truth about astral projection?

Science has been trying to explain paranormal phenomenon like astral projection for centuries with no conclusive findings. It's a heavy field fraught with controversies and disagreements between academics, which makes it difficult to legitimize or debunk any one theory. But when you examine these theories in detail, they can be broken down into two major categories: those purely based in science and those that have spiritual aspects to them.

The first category includes things like lucid dreaming or out-of-body experiences (OBEs). These are experiential phenomena that have traditionally been referred to as "astral projection," but there's no evidence to support the ideas of separating them from sleep and unconsciousness. They're not unique to human beings, but they're not universal either.

OBEs were studied in the 1940s by renowned psychologist William Baldwin. He believed that his subjects were traveling out to other planes of existence like astral projection, and he claimed to have found multiple manifestations of this experience.

However, his studies had a number of flaws. He didn't take into consideration that these OBEs could have been hallucinations caused by fever and neurological issues. They didn't account for the fact that his subjects weren't actually experiencing astral projection or any other form of "astral travel." An interesting observation about these studies is their short-lived popularity: as soon as he published his findings, they became very controversial and soon fell out of favor.

But even if this research were valid, it still wouldn't contradict the spiritual aspect to astral projection, which is what we're going to get into now.

The spiritual aspect of astral projection is based on the belief that we're not limited to our physical bodies. You're free to ignore your body and leave it behind. The most common example of this is something called "traveling" through the third dimension, which is when you suddenly find yourself in a different place, or being able to see matter that's normally invisible.

When you travel through the third dimension, you're actually seeing a part of reality that's under the surface in our world — like underwater, but invisible to human eyes. That's because it exists on another plane of existence.

This theory is based on the idea that beings are capable of existing in multiple dimensions. It's important to note that this isn't just an idea, but rather a reconceptualization of what "dimension" means. This dimension is not just spatial, but it also encompasses time.

A dimension with time is called a brane, and it's what string theory describes our physical reality as: a three-dimensional brane floating in the eleven-dimensional multiverse. But there are other branes we can interact with in other parts of the multiverse too. Some believe our universe is like a bubble universe floating out there somewhere, and these parallel universes can be accessed through astral projection or lucid dreaming. These parallel universes are called "alternate realities" by some.

So is this theory valid? Well, it certainly makes sense in a metaphorical way, but it's still impossible to prove with any kind of scientific rigor.

The second category includes things like teleportation and psychokinesis—the ability to move matter without physical contact. Some of these things can be seen with the naked eye, whereas others require specialized equipment. Teleportation appears to be the most controversial of all: while some people may claim that they've experienced it regularly, you'll find very few scientific studies supporting this phenomenon.

The one study that was conducted showed that the results of a teleporter were consistent with random chance. However, the subjects did have a history of participating in anomalous activity, which is why it's more likely that they were just faking it.

A more unusual example of teleportation is seen in India when people claim to have had the ability to teleport what appear to be animals by making a sound in their ears or through pointing their fingers at the animals. It's still unknown how these "teleportations" work, but they're still referred to as "teleportation" even though there's no evidence to support it.

Psychokinesis is the ability to influence the world around us with your mind. It's based on a set of laws called the "Law of Attraction," which states that you can direct your desire and energy to bring about a certain outcome. The best example of this is in personal development. If you want something in life, you can envision it and, with enough practice, see it appear as if by magic.

This raises a lot of confusion when people try to explain psychokinesis and how it relates to astral projection, because you're not only describing soul travel through different dimensions or universes, but also abilities such as telepathy and precognition. If you're able to somehow physically influence the world around you, couldn't that mean that it's not really a form of astral projection?

Well, we can look at how some people describe astral projection and see if there are any similarities. The most common accounts of what happens when you astral project is that there's a feeling of being "detached" from your physical body. You may suddenly find yourself moving at superhuman speeds and know things before they happen. That's similar to how some people describe having psychic abilities, like knowing about someone else's problems before they happened.

Other people say that they're very aware of the body they're in while they astral project. If you utilize the Law of Attraction, you can direct your energy to go find another body nearby and inhabit it instead. This is like teleporting into a different dimension or universe, but it's a "real" universe in our terms: one we can physically interact with.

Still others have claimed their souls leave their bodies during an OBE and travel through space, interacting with other souls and living a life like on Earth until being recalled by their bodies. If you're able to do that, then it's possible that you could also interact with other beings in another reality as well.

The difference between astral projection and other types of ability is how they're experienced. Astral projection usually happens suddenly when a person's body is lying down, relaxed. This is in contrast to precognition, where the person would typically have to be looking at a static image or reading something without really thinking about it for the information to appear.

The next two categories are abilities we've been talking about throughout this guide: telepathy and precognition. Both of them are considered part of "empathy," which is the ability to read another person's thoughts or emotions. These include things like Reiki, clairvoyance, and telekinesis.

These abilities are generally not as controversial as other abilities because they can be observed in a lab setting. For example, research has shown that we all have the ability to read someone else's mind, which is possible because of the

Law of Correspondence: just as you can think about anything in your physical world, you can also think about anything in your mental or spiritual worlds.

One of the most famous experiments on this subject was conducted at Princeton University. In this study, students were put in separate rooms separated by a curtain and connected by a keyboard and monitor. One person would be asked to play a game of the other's choosing and then answer several questions about the game. They were also supposed to not talk about it with anyone else.

The other person would sit by a computer screen and read the other student's mind and attempt to guess what they were thinking. The experiment was so successful that it won a Ig Nobel Prize, which are given out for research that makes people laugh and then think.

The next two categories are considered "telekinetics," which is the ability to influence matter without physical contact. The most common example of this is psychokinesis, or using your mind to move an object without touching it.

This is actually a good example of how something appears to be one thing when it's actually something else. If you walk into a room and see a chair being moved, it's likely that you wouldn't think "someone is using mind powers on that chair." But if someone tried to move your body without touching it, like by pulling at your hands from across the room, you'd probably realize they were using mental abilities.

One of the most controversial things about psychokinesis is telekinesis, which is the ability to use your mind to move an object without touching it. This has been demonstrated in experiments where people appear to have caused objects to move without touching them. This is considered controversial because you can't observe the ability directly, so it's hard to prove that someone is doing it rather than just saying they are.

People have also claimed that they've had telekinetic abilities since childhood, and some claim that they've had them for much longer than that. Sometimes people who claim to be able to move an object mentally can also see this object moving on their mental screen, like a cartoon being played in front of them. Some people are even able to give a visual representation of the object they're moving without having any physical interaction or knowledge of it.

Some people have actually studied this ability and replicated it in a lab setting. One of the most famous examples of this is the research done at Yale University under Dr. Daryl Bem. He's been studying human intuition and precognition for a long time, and one of his most well-known studies involved asking students to look at a series of word pairs on a computer monitor. These words were supposed to be random, but some word pairs were meant to give the student "correct" answers in relation to other words that would come up later on in the experiment (for example: if "blue" came up as an answer, then "green" would be one you should choose later).

Dr. Bem found that some students were able to predict the word pairs that would be right on the computer screen. The surprising thing was that these students couldn't tell him what they could see on their own minds. They could only describe what they saw on the computer screen, which was a common phenomenon called "blindsight," which is a type of blindness where people are blind to something happening in front of them, but they're still aware of it happening in other ways (like hearing it happen).

WHAT EXACTLY IS ASTRAL PROJECTION?

It is a process of consciously stepping out of one's physical body to explore the world or experience anything without being physically present. The idea that we can leave our physical body at will, and enter into an astral plane as an observer has been around for centuries. It was first brought to the attention of Western Civilization in the 19th century by Theosophy and Spiritualism movements when they were investigating spiritualistic practices such as table-turning and automatic writing.

Astral projection is not considered a fraud but a genuine psychic phenomenon with many anecdotal accounts from credible sources who have claimed to have experienced it. According to mainstream scientific view, it is dismissed as an illusion or hallucination due to the lack of empirical data and researchers in the field of parapsychology prefer instead use terminology such as "out-of-body experiences" (OBEs) to describe the phenomenon.

In a nutshell, astral projection is a process whereby the astral body separates from its physical counterpart and floats freely in higher dimensions. It's also known as an out-of-body experience because you are "out" of body and can travel anywhere you want without being restrained by time or space.

In the context of astral projection, we can break the process down into two steps:

STEP 1: Your physical body is asleep and you are no longer conscious. This is known as sleep paralysis or hypnogogia. You are now in a state where your conscious mind doesn't allow you to move or use normal senses.

STEP 2: As your mind continues to relax and disengage, your consciousness enters a dream-like state which allows you to temporarily separate from your physical body. The separation itself could be instantaneous or it may take minutes, hours or even days depending on the person's experience.

Once you enter the astral plane, your mind becomes your reality. You are free to explore and go anywhere you want without being restrained by time and space. The astral dimension is open for exploration just like our physical reality but has that added element of dream-like phantasmagoria where anything is possible.

The Practice of Astral Projection

Astral projection is a practice that can be practiced at any time and any place. It is completely individual and depends on your ability to enter into the appropriate state of mind, which varies from person to person. The practice involves climbing through three levels of evolution, and by following this seven-stage process, you will succeed in awakening your consciousness. We are going to look at each stage in detail below:

Before we go into detail about the stages of astral projection, it's important to know first what happens when you are asleep.

This is when your brain enters its most active state and physically appears to be awake but you are still in an unconscious state. During the REM stage of sleep you are still capable of performing complex biological and cognitive functions, such as dreaming and motor action. Interestingly, it is during this phase of REM where the mind wakes up while the body continues to sleep.

So what exactly goes on within your mind during this time? Well, a few minutes after you fall asleep, the subconscious mind kicks in and takes over that part of your consciousness which is responsible for generating dreams. This part of your mind has an infinite capacity for imagination and it is during this stage that your mind invents various scenarios to answer questions you may have or solve problems you are facing.

The fact that this portion of your conscious mind is responsible for generating dreams automatically leads to the conclusion that lucid dreaming (sometimes referred to as astral projection) is a lot easier than trying to project out of body during REM (Rapid Eye Movement) sleep since you know exactly when these dreams are going to happen.

In this guide we are going to take a closer look at each stage of astral projection.

You may be asking yourself why we would want to enter into this dream-like state. In the spirit of the cosmic law of cause and effect, dreaming is a prerequisite for manifesting. It may sound like a ridiculous statement but when you think about it, you will realize that manifesting is not something that happens overnight and it cannot be achieved by merely assuming you are going to get what you want.

When you meditate for example, your subconscious mind has the ability to receive and interpret your intentions but this can only happen with deep concentration. The more intense the concentration, the deeper into dream-like state your mind enters. The moment you are immersed in this state, you'll start receiving information that will eventually lead to your desired result.

This dream-like state is also a good place to start channeling information. The channeling of information is based on the fact that your mind has great access to different sections of the astral dimension and you can literally receive information from different astral entities.

SPIRIT: HOW CAN I ASTRAL PROJECTION?

This is not a question you ask yourself when you want to astral project. Instead, you may be asking yourself: "How can I astral project?" It's a legitimate and common question, but the answer is not so simple and straightforward. There are many ways to astral project, but only two methods will guarantee success: through meditation or by having other people do it for you while your physical body sleeps. With these two methods, there are many different variations of what type of meditation or body-soul separation technique will work for each individual person based on their belief system and personal spiritual beliefs. In addition, there are other variations to make astral projection more effective. There are plenty of people out there who have used this knowledge for years, but don't know how to tell someone else how to do it. Our goal is to give you a primer on that basic information and detail some of those variations for you in an easy-to-understand fashion.

First, let's look at meditation. It's a commonly used way of astral projecting because most people have already tried or wanted to try a meditation technique before they learn about astral projection or any other spiritual or metaphysical/new age concepts. Meditations can be done by just sitting still or by using a technique that involves moving around. Usually the student learns the basic meditation techniques with a teacher and performs them under that teacher's guidance. However, if you're serious about trying astral projection, then you might want to do it on your own. In other words, you might want to learn how to do it without the assistance of a teacher or in some cases without any assistance at all. This can be done through meditation courses offered by both major religions (Hindu, Buddhist, etc.), as well as more in-depth methods taught only in certain occult schools or lodges. Or, if you're a skeptic, you can just fool around with astral projection and see what happens. For those of you wanting to do yoga or meditation in general, we recommend the book Astanga Yoga by T.K.V. Desikachar (aka Jivamukti Yoga) as the best place to learn more about meditation techniques from expert teachers who have modeled themselves after Paramahansa Yogananda and Swami Sivananda (See Book Recommendations: Astanga Yoga by TKV Desikachar).

Most people start out doing astral projection through mediation before moving on to another method. Many people say, "I was meditating for a while but I couldn't do it." The answer to that is: you just haven't found the right technique yet. When you first start meditating, it's normal to go through many different techniques before finding the one that "works" for you. The problem is that most of those meditation experiences are not as deep and profound as astral projection, and they often lose their value when done by themselves. Instead of feeling good about yourself for having achieved something spiritually profound like astral projection, people usually just feel frustrated because they didn't do it correctly.

So instead of using meditation to propel their spiritual growth (a slow process), these people progress too quickly to their next stage. Beginners are most impressed with the more mystical, miraculous, and exotic phenomena of astral projection, so it's very tempting for them to skip over meditation altogether. If you do that, then once you learn how to astral project through mediation you'll have a huge advantage because the rest of your training will come much more easily.

This is why we recommend that only beginners first learn through meditation without any outside help. Once you successfully perform astral projection techniques on your own during meditation (or with no guidance), that's when you know they're working for you and can be taken to the next level. For those who are thinking of moving on to another method, we recommend that you don't skip over your first stage of meditation and go straight to the next one. You'll get a better start on success if you wait until you've mastered the most basic meditation techniques before jumping to astral projection. The same goes for any other occult or metaphysical/new age subject.

Now let's talk about the second way to astral project… as a person who is not sleeping at the same time as their physical body. This method has many variations, but the basic idea is that another person uses his or her own mind to project their astral body to your physical location while you sleep. This is a very advanced technique and requires an experienced practitioner of astral projection who knows how to do it. It can be dangerous if things are not done correctly. This is why it's best to learn this technique from a qualified teacher that can help prevent any problems from happening while you are learning it.

As we said earlier, you can learn this method either from books or from people with experience and expertise in the occult art of astral projection. There are many qualified people who can teach this method; we don't know of anyone who can teach this method better than we can.

Now that we've covered the basics of astral projection and the methods for learning it, let's look at some of the things you need to do in order for it to work. We call these things "pre-requisites." You'll know if you have them because once you begin to practice your meditation or whatever method you decided to use, they will come naturally. They will be strong points of wisdom, intuition, and other psychical awareness that will help make your astral projection more successful.

The pre-requisites for astral projection are these:

1) Poise: A general psycho-physical poise, which is a stable and healthy life-style. It's not just physical poise but also psychological and emotional poise. This means you need to do things that keep you healthy, happy, and balanced in your various aspects of life. If you're on a destructive path, you'll find it hard to astral project. If you're not happy where you are, you won't have the motivation to perform your astral projection techniques. If your emotional or mental state gets out of whack, then that will affect your astral projection efforts

as well. This is why we recommend calming techniques such as yoga and meditation to help keep the mind in a stable state of equanimity where it's open to higher consciousness.

2) Emotional detachment: The ability to have a strong emotional detachment from the body. This means you can be in your physical body and sleep while another person is in your astral body doing something else. You won't have any desires or fears about what the other person is doing, because you don't know what he or she is doing. But if you want to know how to astral project as a skill, this is one of the pre-requisites we need to talk about.

3) Deep relaxation and meditation: This means that you need to become very relaxed and calm during your meditation time or practice of yoga/meditation. This allows for the mind to be more receptive and open up for higher consciousness. If you can practice all of the techniques that we teach here on this website to the point that you have become a master at them, you'll achieve a very deep and intense state of relaxation and meditation. Eventually it will feel so good during your astral projection training sessions that you'll think about not wanting it to end!

This is why we recommend that beginners perform basic yogic breathing techniques such as alternate nostril breathing and even Kapalabhati breathing (which helps with pranayama). If these practices are done correctly and to a certain level of proficiency, then they will help push the boundaries of your astral projection abilities. If you want to find out how to do those breathing techniques on this website, you can find them in the "How To" section.

4) A strong, healthy, and balanced life-style: This means that you need to eat a healthy diet, stay physically fit while avoiding over-exertion or stress, and make sure that your mind is clear by clearing your thoughts frequently and not over-indulging in recreational drugs or alcohol. Some people who are astral projecting will say that all of these things are necessary for a successful project. But others simply have abilities that some people do not. So if you're not a teetotaler and still want to astral project, then you'll just have to push yourself harder in your method of choice. It's easy for us to say that we need to be healthy while we sit here in front of our computer writing articles and promoting our website. Staying true to our practices is also something we need to work on!

5) Openness: Openness implies an ability or willingness to be open-minded but it also implies that you are willing or able to "widen" your mind so that you can learn the skills necessary for astral projecting. In other words, you need to be willing to learn new things and try new techniques. Basically, if you want to know how to astral project as a skill, then you must be open-minded.

FULLY CONSCIOUS ASTRAL PROJECTION

Fully conscious astral projection is the act of having a voluntary out-of-body experience at will. In other words, you can take control and leave your body for an extended period of time.

We'll outline some of the first steps you should take with some clarity on why they are important in getting started with astral projection.

If you're ready and you're ready to astral project, then build your bridge to the stars.

There are various techniques available for achieving astral projection, but the bottom line is that all of them require you to build a bridge to the astral plane.

To begin with, make sure you understand the different stages of sleep. In a nutshell: The first stage of sleep is called deep sleep (aka REM). This period lasts from about three or four hours after you fall asleep until about thirty minutes before your scheduled awakening from sleep. During this period, your brain waves slow down and irregular small spasms in the muscles occur intermittently. You also become more and more relaxed. The third stage of sleep (aka Light Sleep) occurs approximately ten minutes before your awakening from sleep, and is characterized by a marked slowing of the brain waves, the muscles are more relaxed, and there are fewer spasms. At this point you may be dreaming, or you may be deep in sleep. The fourth stage of deep sleep (also called true sleep) lasts from ten to ninety minutes and occurs right before you wake up. These brain waves have aroused virtually all the muscles throughout the body – even those not used in daily activity – so that they are completely limp and relaxed (both physically and energetically). This period is also characterized by a marked slowing of respiration and heart rate. The final stage of deep sleep (also called slow-wave sleep) begins about forty-five seconds before the alarm goes off, lasts about thirty seconds or so, and occurs in short surges lasting only a few seconds at a time. This is the only stage of sleep that yields any results!

Anyone who has had a chance to observe this sequence firsthand can attest that it really does go like clockwork! Sleep researchers have confirmed that 95% of all dreams emerge during these stages I to IV (deep sleep).

The reason for this is due to an amazing biological phenomenon called Sleep Paralysis. When we fall asleep, our bodies automatically enter the deepest stage of sleep. However, before we completely fall asleep, our bodies suffer from a bizarre phenomenon called Sleep Paralysis. The reason for this is that as the body is sleeping, it enters a period in-between stage three and stage four. That's when things get weird! When you enter this state it feels like you're awake and experiencing something real.

While you're experiencing Sleep Paralysis it's best to remain still because every time your muscles move your body moves back to the first (light) sleep state! This periods of time can last between ten seconds to several minutes depending on how deep your body has fallen asleep. The goal of astral projection techniques is to get you to surrender completely as your body falls into the deepest state of relaxation.

So, what is the purpose of those weird spasms? Over hundreds of years, people have associated these movements with spirits and supernatural encounters. The truth is that these spasms create an energetic bridge between the physical and astral planes! It's no coincidence that as one falls asleep their body becomes more relaxed (and energy free). So it's really no mystery why our bodies are prone to spasm at this time.

You may have heard of this energetic bridge from yoga or in spiritual practice. The science behind it is simple: your physical body has a high density of electrical energy. If you had an electromagnet, then just as it pulls iron filings to it, your physical body pulls energies towards it!

In addition to this, the astral plane is one hundred times more energetic than the physical plane; therefore, as your body relaxes so does the energy around it. The energetic bridge then acts like a magnet for attracting higher energies towards your body (as you sleep). This creates a bridge between the two planes. It's kind of like how a magnet's pull is stronger in the direction that it's oriented towards. This is why you may have experienced Sleep Paralysis before in your dreams; it's simply an energetic bridge from the physical to the astral world.

As far as what happens during sleep paralysis:

The more relaxed your body becomes, the more easily your mind and inner voice will connect to your subconscious, which then allows you to then enter the astral realm.

For many people this can feel really weird! As you're entering this new reality, it may feel like (and often is) really strange and foreign to have no control over your actions in dreamtime. For others it may feel like you're getting into a car accident, or that your body is falling. Interestingly, this is a recurring theme in the astral realm. We all have seen the movie The Matrix, right? In my opinion this perfectly depicts what it's like to experience sleep paralysis.

So how does one prevent OBEs? It's all about manipulating the state of your body! When you're in control of your body then you control its ability to enter deeper states of relaxation and therefore trigger sleep paralysis and astral projections.

The first step towards achieving this is by mastering the art of Autosuggestion. The goal of Autosuggestion is to allow your subconscious mind to take control over the conscious mind.

Autosuggestion is a technique in which you can use your mind to influence something. It involves making a statement or affirmation, like commanding yourself that you will have an OBE tonight. You may also find autosuggestion helpful in using hypnosis or affirmations while performing relaxation techniques (like Meditation and Binaural Beats).

The key with autosuggestion is to be specific about what you want, and how you want it to happen! What I mean by this is that if you're going to use autosuggestion for astral projection, then do not suggest that "something might happen tonight." Instead, say something like "I will wake up at 10:30 pm tonight and have an out of body experience."

The reason that you want to be specific is because the subconscious mind needs absolute clarity on what it wants to achieve. If you don't have clarity on what you're trying to achieve, then your subconscious mind might think that you're asking for a new cell phone or something like that!

There are many techniques to use autosuggestion, but I personally like to use visualization, affirmations, and visualization combined with music. Visualization works really well because it allows the subconscious and conscious minds to visualize the same thing (I give full instructions on how to do this in my eBook). Affirmations work well if you're in a really relaxed state of mind. The reason is that affirmations involve using your voice and will power as well. This will help you to focus your mind on the positive aspects of what you want to achieve.

It's important that you don't just throw these techniques at your problem. You do not want to use autosuggestion and then just hope for the best, because unless your intention is really clear, then your subconscious mind is likely to associate that it's going to get a new car or something like this. The key is to put in time and effort into learning the techniques and being able to express clearly what you want through them! You can then re-use these techniques in all your daily life situations, whether it be relationships, stress management, addiction, or whatever else comes up.

DIFFERENCE BETWEEN ASTRAL PROJECTION AND LUCID DREAMING

You know what's going on, and while it is often impossible to wake up in a lucid dream, you're typically able to act upon the content of your dreams (e.g., fly or punch holes in walls) rather than just observing them passively.

It's believed that astral projection happens when your consciousness leaves your physical body and enters a dreamscape or another plane outside of the physical world — this process can be done voluntarily. The process is similar to lucid dreaming, except that the astral body is separate from your physical body, rather than being part of it.

Astral projection is something that many believe everyone can do at any time, and many people have reported trying out this discipline. However, there are only a few documented instances of people who have succeeded in creating the ability to travel consciously in their dreams.

Once you've become conscious during dream sleep (i.e., awaken as early as seven or eight hours before you would normally wake up for the day), you can project your consciousness by allowing yourself to enter an altered state of consciousness in which you are consciously aware that you're asleep and dreaming. To help you enter this state, you can try counting up to 20 before telling yourself that you will remain conscious until your attempt is over (this helps stave off sleep for a moment), and then imagine that you are projecting your consciousness into the air. You can also imagine your consciousness leaving your room. To help you keep your attention on this task, it's also helpful to count back from 20 to one while protecting yourself out of your body until you arrive in another location.

For example, you can't fly until you learn how to levitate, a skill which many people claim not to possess. You also can't read someone else's thoughts or feel another person's emotions until you learn the appropriate skill. However, some believe that the lack of specific skills doesn't necessarily stop them from doing anything they want in their dreams.

By taking on extra awareness and consciousness, you could create a very powerful form of hypnosis within your dreams that allows you to perform physical feats. You can project your consciousness to another location or be able to communicate through the senses (see the list below, which provides some instruction on how to do this). You could also use your awareness to create astral matter or use it as a weapon.

According to the website "How to Do It", there are two different forms of astral projection: direct and indirect. Direct projection is when you leave your physical body from within it, and then enter another location by traveling on a beam of light. In indirect projection, you leave the physical body from a location outside of it, which could be outside of your bedroom and at an unknown distance in space. Here's how to enter a dreamscape through direct projection:

As you become familiar with astral projection, you'll be able to tell the difference between dreaming and being awake. You can also leave your physical body while sleeping, without being in a dream, by using your astral form. This is called "waking up" out of body (OBE). First, lie on your back in a relaxed position on the ground or within a bed. Imagine that you're moving up through the bed in the direction of its headboard and the ceiling above it. Once you've reached this point with your consciousness, imagine that you're moving ahead until you reach an area where there's no longer any floor underneath you (i.e., the ceiling). Once you've reached this point, imagine that you're moving ahead a short distance until you come to a barrier. Once you've reached this point, imagine that your astral form is "breaking out" of the barrier.

As you reach the other side of the barrier, you will have entered a dreamscape. It's also possible to enter a dreamscape while dreaming or while awake, but from a different location than your physical body — remember that it's not necessary for the physical body and astral form to be in close proximity to one another (i.e., in bed) if they're both conscious within their own dreams.

You can also use your astral form to read someone else's thoughts or to look into their future. Simply imagine that your consciousness has entered your target person's body in the same way it would enter a dreamscape, and then project your awareness into their psyche. From there, look around to see what you can find out about them!

WHAT PROOF IS THERE OF ASTRAL PROJECTION?

For those who do not believe in the phenomenon, it is difficult to prove that a person has actually made a projection. The best way to show that someone has successfully projected is through the experience of those who were with him or her during the event. These experiences should match up. It is also possible for a person who astral projected to obtain corroborating evidence from his or her out-of-body self. This might include reading something from another room, or something hidden behind them which they could not have seen otherwise.

It is possible for a person to experience things while astral projecting, which does not happen or cannot happen while they are awake. The second type of proof would be an out-of-body experience. The most common OBE involves some form of "out of body" experience in which a person feels as if he or she is flying around the room and sees the room from above, although there might be other experiences such as seeing through walls, observing other people or things, etc. As for traveling to another location, this can also be accomplished through astral projection by using one's imagination and what we call "the power of thought."

To put it simply, astral projection is the ability to travel to other locations and/or non-physical planes of existence while in a dream-like state. When I was a child, I would often have OBEs in my sleep. It was always an amazing experience for me, as I felt as if my body was floating above my bed. I only recently learned about the term "astral projection" and decided that this is what I had been experiencing all of my life. Now that I know more about astral projection, it makes perfect sense to me, as this is a very natural part of life.

There are many things that people recognize as proof of astral projection, such as detailed historical events that occurred before they were born. People who have projected before are often able to repeat these events in the form of a sort of "playback" when they are in the astral state. It is also common for people to remember their past lives or other people's past lives when they project. Many people who project also claim to be in some kind of spiritual dimension, although this could depend on each individual's beliefs. Many who have been exposed to complex religious or spiritual beliefs are able to project to their respective belief system.

In order to prove that astral projection is real, you would need a person who can project, and another person who is fully awake and in the physical state. You would also need an accurate way of measuring time, which could not be distorted (i.e., a clock that cannot be easily tampered with). Another requirement would be an area where there are no disruptions from electromagnetic fields or other surrounding objects. These are some conditions which would allow for the most accurate results when proving this phenomenon.

It is difficult to prove astral projection because of the nature of the experience. A person's consciousness is separated from the physical body during an OBE state. Therefore, it is not like a memory where you can present hard evidence which can be checked against real life events. In order to prove that astral projection is real, you would need a person who can project, and another person who is fully awake and in the physical state. You would also need an accurate way of measuring time, which could not be distorted (i.e., a clock that cannot be easily tampered with). Another requirement would be an area where there are no disruptions from electromagnetic fields or other surrounding objects. These are some conditions which would allow for the most accurate results when proving this phenomenon.

Most of the proof of astral projection is through anecdotal evidence. Through my own experiences, I know that it is possible to have out-of-body experiences. I also believe that many other people have had these same experiences, whether they realize it or not. There will always be naysayers who will discount these experiences because they cannot personally relate to them, but there are so many people who can testify to having one or more out of body experiences.

There are also several scientifically proven cases which lend credence to the reality of astral projection, such as OBE induced by drugs such as ketamine, and schizoprenia.

There were multiple reports of a woman who experiences OBEs and projects herself from one place to another, folding the space in the process. These experiences were verified through interviews and cameras placed in locations where she projected herself from one location to another.

Astral projection has also been discussed by mystics including Chuangzi, Origen, Plotinus, St. Augustine, St. Teresa of Avila, Emanuel Swedenborg , and Sri Yukteswar .

Astral projection was also popularized by Robert Monroe's book "Journeys Out of the Body", which describes his over forty years of experience with these phenomena. Science fiction writer Arthur C. Clarke also wrote about astral projection in his novel "Childhood's End", crediting the concept to the original work of Professor John William Dunne.

John Lilly, a famous oceanographer and neurologist, experimented with his patients by having them project themselves into a tank of water. He reported that "out-of-body experiences" occurred among many of his test subjects.

Interestingly enough, scientists have identified many similarities between the brain during an OBE state and the brain during a dream state. There have been different chemicals found to be released in both states, and both are very similar physiologically. This could lend credence to the claim that when we are dreaming we are actually projecting our consciousness into other locations while we sleep.

Astral Projection and the Collective Unconscious

While this may not be practical for everyone, there are a few different steps that could be taken in order to achieve astral projection. Many of these techniques involve the use of certain drugs or altered states of consciousness. This is something to consider if you would like to try to achieve this on your own by yourself. The various aspects of astral projection discussed above are:

First, one must learn how to induce oneself into an OBE state through meditation or other techniques. You can also learn how to induce an OBE state more quickly through various methods such as deep breathing exercises and visualization. The OBE state is different from a lucid dream state in that it is more similar to being conscious in the physical world where you are aware of your surroundings, and can observe yourself. There is also the phenomena known as Astral Form Projection, where you create an energy or dream body that stays while your physical body sleeps. This means you can actually get up and walk around through this projection, which may be easier for some people than achieving the full separation of consciousness from the physical body.

This second form of astral projection is also more like lucid dreaming, except that it does not end when you wake up in the morning. I would definitely recommend practicing projection in your dreams before trying to achieve it while you are awake.

ADVANTAGE OF ASTRAL PROJECTION

When you practice astral projection, there are many benefits that come with it. For one, you are able to visit the world of your dreams; furthermore, you can create a sanctuary where there is beauty and peace no matter how chaotic your physical life might be. There is also the spiritual release that comes from connecting to a higher plane of consciousness. Sure it sounds all too good to be true, but these benefits exist in astral projection for sure! The more practice you get with this spiritual tool the better off your well-being will be as well.

As a break from reality and meditation as a restorative substitute on top of being an interesting experience, astral projections have many great advantages. Getting out of your mundane life and into the alternative world of the astral plane is a great way to take some time to reevaluate your life. You can discover what really affects you and what you are truly passionate about, then use that information when you return.

Properly practicing astral projection will allow you to move past some problems that may have been present in the physical realm. Maybe there was a relative in the family that had passed away, or an ex-partner who has caused you trouble, or maybe just a bad day at work.

Astral projection can be a very beneficial exercise as well. In the astral plane, you are able to visit places in your dreams that may never have been experienced before. This can be a great way to unlock creativity and bring about new ideas. It's also a great way to see beauty that is always present but unseen by most people because they can't afford a second home in the astral plane.

Astral projection has many spiritual advantages as well, especially when you are able to connect with positive spirits from another realm of existence. You will have a greater appreciation for life and receive excellent advice from those who are enlightened in the spiritual realm who have achieved total consciousness of the universe around them.

WHAT IS THE EASIEST WAY TO ASTRALLY PROJECT?

Before you attempt to astrally project, it is important to know the different methods that are available. One of the easiest ways to astrally project is with the use of entheogens, or plant substances that can produce altered states of consciousness and sometimes spiritual experiences, such as mushrooms. These substances promote peace and tranquility which helps one relax while visualizing an astral body outside of their physical body. This method is fairly easy to do for beginners but only works for those who have already mastered meditation and/or relaxation techniques since you need both mental clarity and an empty mind in order for this technique to work properly.

In order to project and create a physical body in the astral realm, one must be 100% honest with themselves and prepared to deal with the repercussions. This means you must be ready to face your fears, mental images of past life traumas, and negative thoughts such as "what if it doesn't work?" or "what if I fail?" An honest projection into the astral realms is not for those who want an easy way out. Astrally projecting can be a very dangerous practice. The mind in this case is capable of doing things that it would not normally do while awake in the physical body. This is why it is important to feel completely comfortable with yourself and your surroundings before attempting an astral projection.

Another easy way to astrally project is through the use of technology. Another device which works similarly is called Hemi Sync or binaural beats technology. This method uses a pre-recorded audio track containing two different frequencies, one each played in each ear by headphones. This technology is very effective but it takes a bit of time to become acquainted with it since you may find yourself confused or sleepy during the early stages of this technology.

The most common method used by beginners is via meditation and relaxation techniques. This method can be done through physical methods such as yoga, tai chi, and bodywork or through metaphysical methods such as trance music or mantras which help one achieve a complete state of relaxation. More experienced meditators and those familiar with these techniques can accomplish astral projection without any difficulty.

Naturally, the easiest time to astrally project is if you are alone in a room with no distractions and at a time when your mind is completely clear. There are two main types of meditation that can be used for this purpose: formal meditation and silent meditation. A formal meditation would be one done on the floor with your eyes closed while sitting in a comfortable position and chanting certain words or sounds out loud such as "Om", "Aum", or "Hallelujah". A silent meditation would be done while lying down or sitting upright on the floor in complete silence. These activities are important and necessary in order for you to reach the appropriate state of mind.

Once the necessary conditions have been met, one must then focus on what they want to accomplish. Focusing on a specific goal while astrally projecting is essential because if you do not set an explicit goal while astral projecting it would be much harder to accomplish. When using entheogens, one must use their full attention to keep all thoughts at bay and not find themselves in a fantasy world where they can live out their wildest fantasies. One must also use them sparingly so that you don't become too over-excited and create a wild imagination that can interfere with your astral projection.

Once you have attained a state of near enlightenment, it would be wise to begin clearing out your mind of thought patterns such as thoughts that are negative, obsessive, or that cause you to feel uncomfortable. Another way is to sit quietly for a while and simply think about nothing at all which will help you return to your physical body.

Once one has returned from their astral adventure they should become more conscious during this time period. Most people usually wake up with a profound sense of calmness and would feel like they've been on vacation without having gone anywhere. They usually feel like they have just returned from a very deep sleep and when they open their eyes they cannot remember anything except for their last thought or feeling which is usually something that was disturbing, such as pain or something that was difficult to deal with, or finding themselves in a dangerous situation.

Try not to stay outside of yourself or in a fantasy world. It is recommended that one stay conscious until all the effects from the entheogen have worn off which can take up to half an hour.

Metaphysical energy is the life force itself, that which is directly connected to our soul. This life force is known in many pagan traditions as God, or the Divine Feminine. The energy of this Divine Feminine is what keeps us alive and well in physical form. When one's consciousness is completely separated from her this Divine Feminine can become blocked bringing about ill health in the physical body.

Many people who are new to astral projection will find themselves having a difficult time focusing on their future when travelling into their past lives. Even some advanced astral projectors have difficulty in this area. The reason for this is because when a person projects into their future they usually find themselves surrounded by a multitude of different goals and desires that they are trying to achieve. These types of situations can be very distracting and it would be easy to lose your focus while trying to accomplish them all.

Until one has learned how to separate themselves from their material body and gain a state of true enlightenment, learning to use the power that the Divine Feminine brings is extremely important. This is why it is highly recommended that you familiarize yourself with metaphysics and astrology so that you can understand how the energy flows throughout your physical body which will help you better utilize this life force power.

Once you have mastered the art of focusing, using your astral body, and understanding how this life force energy works then you can begin to attempt to project out of your physical body. This is a dangerous process and it would be wise to only do this with a full knowledge of what you are doing. The most common methods used for this purpose are through trance-like states such as those found in entheogens or through meditation that results in a state of contemplative awareness.

Astrally projecting is more than just dreaming within our physical body. It is actually an effortless process that we use to temporarily leave our physical form while staying consciously aware of our surroundings. This makes it possible for us to turn our attention elsewhere while leaving our physical body still aware of what is happening. It also allows for a full sensory experience while still in the physical body.

Many people have heard about astral projection but may not be sure exactly how or even what it is all about. These terms are often used interchangeably but there are actually many differences between them. Astral Projection can be defined as the act of leaving ones physical body and creating a clear, direct pathway between themselves and their astral form. This is in order that they can travel to another place and live out their life virtually without having to physically travel anywhere.

Astrally projecting is a highly desirable skill to develop over time. This is because it allows the person who knows how to astral project to experience many different things and leave their body at will. This is done by separating their consciousness from their physical body so that they can explore other places in the world or even in the universe without having to physically go anywhere. Astrally projecting is not just for people who are interested in paranormal activities but can also be used by people who just want an escape from life as we know it.

WHAT ARE ALL THE THINGS YOU CAN DO WHILE HAVING AN ASTRAL PROJECTION?

Astral projection is a state of consciousness in which the physical body is asleep and the spirit has detached itself from the body. It can take place through meditation, sleep, or with the use of drugs like peyote. Other forms such as lucid dreaming, out-of-body experiences and near death experiences are similar though much shorter in term. The term astral means "of the stars" and originates from ancient Greece.

Astral projection is, in essence, an out of body experience. While you are in this state you can physically view yourself lying in bed. This experience will be unlike any other you ever had before as it shatters any perceived notions on life we are familiar with as well as the way we perceive ourselves. It is a very positive experience but it can be very dangerous if you do not know what you are doing.

An astral projection can happen at any moment. It can happen while you are asleep or while you are awake. Some people will experience it when meditating or when they're in a dream state. But, sometimes people will project themselves out of their body without any catalyst and these occur very rarely. Basically, astral projection is a state of consciousness that takes place when the physical body is asleep and the spirit has detached itself from the body.

An out of the body experience (OBE) is an experience that usually occurs when the person has just died and their spirit is separated from their physical form. It can happen afterwards as well, but usually it takes place right after a person passes away.

1. What you are experiencing in astral projection is a temporary liberation from your body...

This means that your physical body isn't doing anything while your spirit has left it. As such, this state can be very easy to achieve and go through as all you need to do is disconnect your spirit from your physical form. This can be done by constantly thinking about leaving your physical body and then making it happen. This is why you should pay attention to what is happening if you are doing this at night.

2. but this also means that the original energy in your body is still there...

Astral projection will always leave some trace of its energy in your body. But, this energy will appear in a new form that will normally include an idea or a feeling. These feelings can be very useful for you as they may help you with understanding yourself in a way you hadn't thought possible before or with formulating something new. This energy has also been known to increase creativity and confidence... as well as giving you some of the best ideas for life. Thus, if you get an idea while you are astral projecting it is very likely that you can turn it into something real.

3. But, things aren't always what they seem...

In order to understand what is going on in astral projection, we usually need to look at the physical body and see how it reacts. It will react by trying to bring its energy back so that we know we are still alive and still have a physical body. The original energy in the physical body will react by trying to "pull" us back into our body. The moment after this happens astral projection ends... and the original energy will collapse and eventually leave the body. As such, it may happen that a person has astral projected with the intention to do one thing, but what happens instead is something totally different.

4. For example you will have an astral projection and then you will see a room...

A common experience of astral projection is seeing a room in your mind... or being in a room altogether. This usually happens right when you project away from your physical form and because of this some people think they're in their own bed or have "broken out" of their physical body into some sort of strange vision. But, this is not the case. All you have to do is find a wall or some kind of landmark and see what happens from there. If you do this you will find out that everything else around you is imaginary...

5. and nothing in your room will change...

Astral projection does not affect the physical body at all. It will always remain the same regardless of what happens outside of it. For example, when you astral project your physical body won't start flying or running around with its eyes closed while laughing uncontrollably like we see in cartoons or movies (assuming it is lying in bed). This is something that has never happened to anyone before so there's no reason for it to happen now.

6. You will be able to see yourself from anywhere...

This is where the second part of astral projection comes in. Your physical body may be sleeping or doing something else, but you will still be able to see your physical form from afar. This is not something that we can normally do and thus the way we conceive of an astral projection is different than how it actually is. Usually, when the physical body falls asleep it stops moving and staying awake for a long period of time causes it to move on its own as if it has been drugged or hypnotized (which sometimes help with getting out of this body).

7. You normally see a person as though they have their arms under their head...

This happens a lot when astral projecting. It is even possible for you to stay in another place for a long time and this can happen while you're dreaming, meditating or simply lying on your bed with your eyes closed. But, the reason why so many people see themselves in such a position is because they actually are doing this in real life. However, it is less common to have someone hold their arms under their head while sleeping and thus we find out that what we normally experience during sleep or meditation are two different things. Still, if you do this the most common manifestation of astral projection will happen...

8. When you hold your arms under your head like that it usually means that you are tired...

Astral projecting is a very exhausting experience and because of this the chances of holding your arms under your head are commonly associated with it. But, this should not be the case. When astral projecting your body is still in a state where it can be tired or relaxed and you can do something to change how you feel. If you hold your arms under your head then you will get tired which means that you need to try and move them away from this position. This will usually imply that you are doing something else at that moment...

9. The reason why many people hold their arms under their head like this is because they want to sleep...

We've already mentioned that astral projection is a very exhausting experience. And, when you're tired your body may feel like it wants to sleep for a while. The reason why people hold their arms under their head when they sleep is because they want to rest. But, this has nothing to do with astral projecting or with what we normally think about such experiences. The truth is that holding your arms under your head can make you tired and you may accidentally fall asleep as though you were any other normal person sleeping on the bed. We won't say this doesn't happen because there are many cases of people waking up on the floor and not knowing how they got there...

10. Astral projection and physical body sleep have nothing in common...

Astral projecting is very different from sleep and they are two separate things. The fact that you hold your arms under your head while you sleep has nothing to do with astral projection and because of this it is normal for someone to think about one thing just before falling asleep. For example, if you sync into the astral before going to bed then it is possible that an image of this will appear in your mind before you actually go to sleep. This is almost like having an email notification pop up in front of you right after falling asleep and thus it may startle a person who has something on their mind. There's no reason for this to happen and there is no way of knowing when it will happen.

CAN YOU GET STUCK OUT OF YOUR BODY IF YOU ASTRAL PROJECT?

The answer to this question is a definite no. It's simply a way for your consciousness to leave your body in order to explore the world around you from an "out-of-body" perspective.

That said, this activity is virtually guaranteed to cause you to lose sleep and get incredibly concerned about your own state of mind.

The process of "astral projection" is a physical one. It's the result of a brain wave pattern that occurs during deep sleep and causes you to experience vivid (and frightening) dreams, as well as wake up with the sensation that you have actually left your body.

As such, the only way to "get stuck" out of your body is if you are in fact dreaming that you're stuck.

So, what exactly is "astral projection"? Many people believe that there are two different types of astral projection: partial and complete. However, there really isn't a difference between them. It's just a matter of how close your dream world seems to be to reality.

A partial astral projection is when you feel like you'll be able to leave your body at any time. You're able to see and interact with things around you, albeit not in the same way we do. It's a feeling of being watched, but not actually being "observed," as if there is some form of barrier between yourself and the outside world.

You can focus your attention on one particular room or object. However, if a particular item, person, or conversation catches your interest then it will become an anchor for your awareness. In this sense, it's like going into a hypnosis trance. You are unable to draw your attention away from the anchor, no matter how hard you try.

A full-body experience is a bit different. Instead of being able to just zoom in on one point, you are fully aware that you've left your body behind. You might see yourself lying on the bed or couch and feel like you can walk out of a locked room or door.

How to Astral Project: The Process

There are several ways to "get stuck" out of your body. Some of these methods are practiced by people who know how, while others may be easier when you experience them yourself. Either way, the general process is the same: relax, go into deep relaxation, and then begin to move your awareness away from your physical body.

The most important aspect of this is that you must choose an anchor for your awareness to focus on. In other words, you need a method to both relax and get into a state in which you feel like you're leaving your physical self behind.

To accomplish this, you will want to either focus on a single object or a single person. If you're able to only see one thing, then try standing in the room from which you are projecting yourself. Take notice of how things look and feel. Are these the same as the physical world? Is it possible for you to walk into that room? Find something outside of your body to focus on. If a person is nearby, try moving your awareness toward him or her. Look at their body and face closely — what does your "astral" self actually see?

It's important to realize that even though you may experience an out-of-body situation, your consciousness is not actually separated from your physical self. You are still asleep or unconscious, but your dream is so realistic that you can "leave" your body.

When you have found something in the room that wants to be your focus of awareness, it will be the point from which you will start to astral project. Simply relax more and begin to move your awareness toward the thing you've chosen as an anchor. The process of leaving your body becomes easier with each attempt. You will experience a sense of floating around the room (or whatever object or person has become associated with this particular state).

The reality is that this will probably feel uncomfortable for you at first, and it may take up to half an hour for you to achieve full control over this new state of awareness. You may even feel nauseous.

What to Do if You Astral Project

If you are experiencing a full-body projection, there are some steps you can take to prevent yourself from feeling trapped in the astral plane. If this is something that comes easily to you (and you know how) then it may well be possible for you to wake up and have your consciousness return to your body before long.

The first thing to do is get out of bed as soon as possible. This will simply cause you to get stuck in the astral world and can make the process of waking up more difficult.

Once you go back to sleep, you will have the opportunity to return back to your physical body. If this happens, then try setting an alarm for five minutes. Having this as a clock-in reminder (with two-minute warning) should allow you time to wait until the alarm goes off, before returning to your body.

If you're unable to get out of bed and back to your body in that time frame, try to focus on something other than yourself. Find obstacles in the room or objects that you may have been looking at. Try focusing on them until you feel like you've moved into some sort of astral body. This is your subconscious trying to get rid of whatever made you feel sick or nauseous from leaving your body the first time around.

Once you are consciously aware that you are no longer an astral projection, then focus on walking back down the stairs (it's easier if there are more than two). Once you are in your room again, try to power through the rest of the night like nothing happened.

When it comes to dealing with a full-body projection, there is no reason to be scared. Make sure you are in control of what's happening by keeping yourself clearheaded and alert. Remember that even though these experiences are common and can be very helpful to some people, others may not choose or know how to use this particular method.

The only way that you will be able to get rid of an astral body is if you decide to consciously leave it behind. If you happen upon an obstacle in your room or within your physical body, simply visualize yourself leaving this astral plane and reentering your physical self. This will be the key to allowing your body's inbuilt GPS system to guide your consciousness back into your body before going out again.

Remember that there is no reason to be scared because you're not alone. We have all done this before, and it's normal for our physical bodies to want us to return after we leave them while we sleep. Many people have never experienced this feeling of separation from their physical bodies, but that doesn't mean that it isn't happening all the time while they are asleep at night. It's just a matter of being aware of what is going on in order for us to choose where we want to go when it comes time for us to leave our bodies behind.

Final Thoughts

Some people will never have the ability to experience an out-of-body experience. It's often a skill that is developed only after a person has had more than a few NDEs (near death experiences). This is something that doesn't happen overnight, and it can take years for some people to achieve their very first astral projection. The process of learning how to do this (much like anything else in life) can be difficult at times, but it can also bring many advantages into your life if you are one of the lucky ones who are able to remember what happens while you're out, without waking up at the same time.

CAN A NEGATIVE SPIRIT GO AGAINST OUR WILL IN THE ASTRAL REALM (WHILE I'M ASTRAL PROJECTING)?

Absolutely. The astral realm is one of the places where we are vulnerable, and negative forces know how to take advantage of that. However, it is possible to protect yourself from these forces with knowledge of how they work and by shielding/quarantining their attacks with your own spiritual energy.

When I talk about astral travel, I'm generally talking about consciously leaving your physical body and going into the astral realm. Sometimes this is called "astral projection" or "out of body experience." It is not that difficult to do, but it does require some mental preparation and the right state of mind as well as practice. It also requires a good knowledge of spiritual things and how things work in the astral realm.

In any case, in order to be more aware and more capable in the astral realm, you must develop one or all of your own senses there. There are other senses besides vision, hearing, smell and touch. There is the sense of knowing or sensing. There is the sense of identifying something by its spiritual essence or being able to see in your astral vision things that aren't visible to the physical eye.

There are also psychic abilities that allow you to "read" people and discern their true intentions and what they are feeling. As a general rule, anything that can be done in the astral realm can be done in the physical realm; however, it will take more effort on your part (as it will feel heavier).

It may be easier for me to illustrate this by telling you about one of my own experiences with it. In the summer of 2001, I was doing the usual astral traveling that I've done many times over the years. This was done to keep myself from being so tired that it would take me longer to do things or come back into my physical body after leaving it.

I practiced sun salutations until my legs were completely numb and felt like they were about to fall off from fatigue. After I finished, I lay on the floor for several minutes resting from all the vigorous exercise I had just done. It felt like I was in the most peaceful place in the world.

All of a sudden, I became aware that someone else was in the room with me when I heard what sounded like a deep sigh. This would have been completely normal if it had been one of my family members or someone else who was visiting. The problem was, no one was there except for me! It took me a minute to figure out what this could be. Then, I realized that maybe it was someone who had passed over and had come to visit me. This can be a problem for someone like me who doesn't understand how to interact with them.

This particular entity didn't immediately realize my presence either and kept repeating over and over again in an agonizing low whisper, "Come back to me...Come back to me...Come back...to me..."

In all honesty, I was rather nervous about the whole situation (and still am when it happens). However, this wasn't the first time I had heard the voice of a spirit and wasn't expecting too much. After a few more seconds of it repeating itself and desperately trying to attract my attention, I thought it best to ask, "Who are you?"

The spirit didn't immediately answer, but instead continued to repeat its plea in an even more desperate tone. Finally after what seemed like an eternity of this going on (but was probably half a minute at the most), the spirit responded in its ghostly whisper.

"It's me...It's me...I told you! I told you! Why won't you come back to me? I need you. I need my love. I want it back. I need you. Come back to me...Come back to me...Come back to me...."

This was the first time I was able to speak with someone who had passed over, and it was a strange experience. Through this spirit, I could feel a tremendous amount of emotion and love from him for his twin flame that had passed away years ago in a car accident (we were twins). It was this connection that had brought him to me.

I wanted to know more about his love for his twin flame and what it meant for him. I began to ask some questions, but he kept repeating over and over in an agonized whisper,

"Please...Please...Please...When are we going to be together?"

The first thing I thought was, "Who is this person? It isn't you. This is not you. You are dead. I'm the one who is dead...This is not you. Why can't you understand that?"

I explained to him that even though he was a spirit, he was a spirit of an individual that had passed over long before I had, and we were like different people altogether. It really made me uncomfortable because, even though his twin flame had passed away years ago in the accident, I still felt like he was distracting me from my astral projection and that he didn't seem like what he portrayed himself to be when I first heard him: a dead spirit of one of his loved ones who had passed over long before me.

After many more seconds of his frustrated whispers and pleading, I told him to go away and leave me alone. I was really beginning to feel sleepy from my astral travel and wanted to come back into my physical body. With that, he finally left me alone.

I continued doing the sun salutations for a few more minutes before coming back into my physical body, but I was so exhausted from the exercise I couldn't perform them at all. The energy he had given off had made me feel tired. Even though there was no evidence of anything spiritual in nature in the room at the time (i.e., no feeling, sight or sound), I had an overwhelming sense of connection with this spirit. It was like a part of me wanted to go back to him. I would later learn that this is what happens when you are in an astrally vulnerable state, and I'll go into that later in the book.

I decided not to tell any of my family or friends about this experience because they would probably think I had lost my mind. Something like this happens for some people after an astral projection, but it's rare because most people don't know enough about being in an astral body or how it works with the physical body to understand such an experience. However, if you do experience such a thing, please know that there is hope for you with your spiritual abilities. This could also be a sign for you that you will develop them later on in your life. There are many more psychic abilities than just the ability to have an out-of-body experience. I will go into this in greater detail later on in the book.

I have since learned that when this happens, it usually means that the person who is dead actually exists as a spirit and has not yet moved on to another more evolved plane of existence. This had never happened to me before, but the spirit seemed to believe that he was alive (even though he wasn't) and it was my twin flame that had passed away and still existed as a spirit, not this actual individual who was calling out to me through him. This was explained in greater detail by Kristine McKenna in the book, Extraterrestrial Encounters and their Paranormal Explanations.

WHAT HAVE YOU EXPERIENCED DURING AN ASTRAL PROJECTION?

Some people claim that their lives are completely shattered upon death. Others say they travel to different places and meet other beings. Still others say that they have an experience of being "at one with the universe" or feel connected to everything, lost in a vast sea of energy.

Just as there are many experiences reported after death, there are just as many experiences reported during an astral projection - depending on how it starts, whether you're going for a short or long distance trip, what kind of entity your project in particular with, how you take the exit from your body's physical form and so on.

The astral projection experience is extremely vast and difficult to describe because people often report having a multitude of different experiences. It's not unusual to hear about the same person reporting different experiences each time they project.

Notable differences between these experiences are:

Bodily ailments or injuries during an astral projection are generally quite painful and will be felt in the projected body. With practice, a projector can learn to "take flight" from their body as quickly as possible so as to avoid physical damage while outside their body.

A common misconception is that an astral projection will be absent of all physical senses. While we're conscious in the waking state, our sense of hearing can detect sound waves and our sense of smell can detect chemicals in the air. These senses are also present in the astral plane, thus allowing us to hear and feel things normally.

Many people experience real time whilst projecting - meaning that events happening around them while they are projected may be sensed just as if they were acutely awake and present within their physical body. The astral body may be able to sense the physical plane in a similar way to how we are able to sense the astral plane.

A more advanced skill is being able to project while being consciously aware. This allows you to still have control of your projected body, and you are also technically not asleep. Not being able to hear while projecting can also be seen as a form of protection for yourself and others around you if your mind was still awake.

Projecting into the future can be dangerous, especially if you don't know what is going to happen in the future. Therefore, it's important to prepare yourself before a projection. This should include knowing how to project in a safe way, being knowledgeable about how your projected body will feel during and after a projection, and practicing your techniques before you go out for real.

The first task when projecting is getting out of the physical body safely which is quite simple as long as you are familiar with how it feels to do so and know where your exit point is or was.

Astral Projection can be made much easier if a person has some knowledge about what they are doing and is not afraid of doing it. Knowing your limits is the first step to learning this skill.

The most common methods used to initiate a projection are as follows:

Many people leave their body naturally, which is why the projection is referred to as an OOBE. There are two popular ways of getting out of your body:

The third method is slightly more complicated. Some people follow this method before they practice the first two. Others prefer to follow only the second technique and use both techniques together after learning them well as a projection technique. For example, one may learn how to project by falling asleep and having an OOBE where they wake up at one point and are outside their body. This experience shows that projecting can be made easier by trying methods other than falling asleep, which can be dangerous for inexperienced projectors.

Some of these methods are also used for astral travel and for a projection to occur it is necessary to leave your body in one way or the other. For this reason, it is important to know when you are out of your body. Here are some common symptoms you may experience when you're out:

Many people who practice Astral Projection tend to have difficulties after they wake up from the projection itself.

Astral Projection can also be done with the help of hallucinogenic drugs.

The most common kind of dreams is a semi-conscious lucid dream, where the dreamer knows they are dreaming, but is not fully conscious that they are dreaming. When one wakes up from a lucid dream, they may have trouble remembering what happened or part of it. If an astral projection occurs during a lucid dream, it may be difficult to recall all of the events that took place in the projection or before and after it. The experience may not seem as vivid as other people experience, because you are no longer fully conscious in your physical body and may not have full control over your senses (such as sight and hearing.

Another way to practice Astral Projection is to use Clairvoyance. To do this, people must first utilize their intuition and trust it. They are then able to see objects or events that will take place during the day through the use of clairvoyance. It is important for people that wish to practice astral projection that they possess a strong intuition in order for them to be able to see things directly through clairvoyance. Also, caution must be exercised in order to avoid being exposed to any negative forces or occurrences.

If one plans on practicing astral projection for the first time, one must proceed with caution. There are several things that should be done before a first time projector decides to dive into it. Most people who practice astral projection begin by learning the basics of how their body feels and looks when they are out of their body and are able to move around freely without being bound by gravity. This will help them become more familiar with this type of activity and will allow them to be more prepared when they decide to do it for the first time.

It is also important to have a basic understanding of how the astral plane works before beginning a first time astral projection. This knowledge will help one to be better prepared for this type of experience and will allow them to be more confident in what they are about to embark on. It will also allow them to know what they may experience during this type of activity and will allow them to be better prepared for that occurrence.

It is not recommended that one attempt Astral Projecting while alone. If you attempt it by yourself, it might seem like something has gone wrong if you find yourself unable to call on other spirits or if you cannot see them. Projecting can also be dangerous if one is not properly prepared, so it is best to seek the help of a professional who will be able to guide and assist you in this type of activity. Many people practicing astral projection use a form of meditation for relaxation before attempting this activity which is known as Astral Projection Meditation. This type of ritual can help one to relax and prepare themselves for an astral projection.

Projectors may face different problems after they are out of their bodies. Some problems include, but are not limited to hallucinations, nightmares, or any other kind of unwanted occurrence that they experience after they leave their physical body.

Disconnected emotions and thoughts are another problem that may surface if the projector does not select their own destination. If the projector is in a random location, they may encounter many environments with different forms of energy. One can be confused about where they should go and what they should do in order to survive or even adjust to their new surroundings. They may also feel alone because they will not be able to communicate with anybody who may be present in that place. This is also a dangerous occurrence because one's physical body cannot handle the stress of having no one with them all of the time. Somebody else would have to take over for the projector if this occurs or it can lead to death of the astral projector.

Some people even say that they have difficulty sleeping or have trouble getting to sleep after they are back in their physical body. This can be caused by the feeling of returning to one's physical body and brain, because the mind has to readjust itself to the situation. Sometimes it is difficult for certain people to return back to their physical bodies because they feel more comfortable in the astral plane than in their physical bodies. This leaves them with a feeling that they are not at home when they're in their bodies and it may be hard for them to fall asleep or remain asleep throughout the night.

BENEFITS OF ASTRAL PROJECTS

Astral projections allow you to explore the world in a whole new way. With just your imagination, you can visit a variety of places and cultures that you might not otherwise be able to experience.

-It can also lead to spiritual development. By venturing outside of your physical body, astral projection helps you achieve higher awareness and understanding of yourself and the world around you.

-Astral projects enable an escape from reality or an escape from physical pain. For people who are suffering from illness, accidents or injury, these out-of-body experiences offer relief with some mental distance which eases suffering in the present moment.

-Astral projection can also be used as a form of past life regression therapy. By projecting outside of your physical body, you are able to experience a past life from an entirely different perspective.

-You can also use astral projection for lucid dreaming. If you are an avid lucid dreamer, this type of out-of-body experience can help you learn to control and direct your dreams more effectively.

Astral projections can have their drawbacks as well:

-If you do not know how to project safely or properly, the experience can be frightening or overwhelming.

-A lack of control during an out-of-body projection can cause severe physical damage. For example, if you were to fly while in a dream state, you might accidentally collide with a tree or building and be injured by the impact.

DRAWBACKS OF ASTRAL PROJECTS

Astral projection is a spiritual practice in which people are able to separate their spirit from their physical body. Some of these reasons may include healing, knowledge, or communicating with the universe. However not all of these trips are positive because there can be negative consequences as well.

Astral projection can also be very dangerous because there is no guarantee that a person will always have protection spiritually while they are out-of-body. This could lead to danger of evil spirits or other dangerous entities. An example of this would be if a person was in a dark place and evil spirits tried to take control of their body. The entity could attack the person's astral body as well as their physical body. These spirits may also possess people's bodies in order to torment them for their deeds while they were alive on Earth.

Many people desire to be able to astral project because they think that it will give them access to information that they cannot get while on Earth. However most of these excursions are completely wasted because the information that is obtained is almost always false and not true at all.

It is possible to take astral trips that are very dangerous. Some people are able to leave their body and float off into the air with no protection at all. A person may not know they have left their body until it has been a while later when they can be found in a ditch or behind trees. These astral encounters could be very frightening because if there is an encounter with evil spirits a person's body could also be possessed by themthere are also times when some people can feel as though they are being watched by others while out-of-body. This could be a result of someone's body being possessed without their knowledge.

Finally astral projections can be used to cause problems for others. An example of this would be if a person was trying to take an astral trip with the goal of causing harm to another individual. Someone may do this by possessing the body of that person and then do things that seem completely out-of-character for that person

PREPARING FOR ASTRAL PROJECTS

Preparing for astral projects is about building that mental and physical fortitude to see you through whatever may occur. It's about developing a unique mindset that keeps your consciousness elevated while putting yourself in the best position possible for the experience. From active imagination to meditation, these activities in combination will assist you in getting there.

When it comes to building the mental fortitude, you must first accept that spontaneous OBEs are the result of shattered beliefs and assumptions. Since we're creatures of habit, we've become accustomed to our physical bodies and the sense of comfort they provide.

Certain concepts are fundamental to astral projection; such as your non-physical body being an exact replica of your physical one. In actuality, the similarities end there. Your projected body is an energy-based entity. Now, take that number from your physical body and multiply it by 10 billion. That's how much energy your projected body contains.

Breaking Free From Physical Modifications

Waking up as a projection begins with the mindset of a lucid dreamer. In essence, this means you'll be dreaming that you are awake. Upon gaining awareness of the situation, your conscious mind will become conscious of your non-physical body. Next, you will find yourself in a completely different environment than you left behind.

It all sounds simple enough until we delve deeper into the experience and try to pinpoint what might occur. The human body has been modified to such an extent that it becomes very difficult to explain specific physical sensations and events as they pertain to the astral plane.

For instance, if you felt pain on the physical plain while projecting, you would feel that same pain while in the astral realm as well. It's the same way if your physical body felt pleasure. While you're projecting, the astral body is still connected to its physical counterpart, so whatever happens on one plane will also happen on the other.

The best way to combat this is not an easy method. It's one that requires vigilance and effort in order to yield results. There are many different approaches to achieve results. For starters, it begins with understanding energy and how it flows within your body and out into the environment. Awareness of energy flow is a great step toward creating a bridge capable of transporting you from one plane to another....

Since we are so heavily influenced by what we see, touch, smell, hear and feel, it becomes difficult to lose the perception that our physical bodies are still with us while we are projecting.

This can be a very challenging part of the process. It can take months or even years before you finally break free from your physical shell. Just remember, each day contains 24 hours and one of those hours will be spent as a projection. Therefore, the more you work at it and the longer you take to complete your project, the greater the odds are of a successful outcome.

Like anything else in life, patience is a virtue. It will help pave the way for transforming your physical body into a non-physical body capable of incredible feats....

Escaping the Material World: Advanced Techniques for Projection

It's impossible to experience everything that astral projection has to offer if you only know how to project one dimensionally. Once you learn advanced techniques, there are many more opportunities for you to explore other dimensions and regions entirely. This advanced knowledge will provide you with limitless capabilities while operating within the astral plane.

There are specific exercises for projection, such as how to project consciously, or even how to project on command. These exercises will help you leave your body during sleep and experience the astral plane in a number of ways. They will provide you with abilities you never thought possible....

Now that you know the basics, it's time to learn something new. We begin by exploring the notions of how to consciously and successfully project within any environment. First off, it goes without saying that all methods are capable of achieving successful projections. It depends on what works for you and for what environment you wish to travel in....

In order to successfully project, you must first learn how to dissociate your consciousness from your physical body. Do this by imagining yourself in the astral plane and then trying to feel it. Feel the difference between the two planes as you move around. Move through walls and travel up, down, left and right until you find yourself in a completely different environment than what you left behind....

To travel into the depths of space, locate a star that is within your viewing area. Imagine yourself traveling along with that star, allowing it to take you on a journey out of sight. Once you've traveled far enough away, exit the star and move into outer-space....

Once you have gained the ability to travel in and out of bodies, you might want to consider entering the dream state from a conscious perspective. The first step in achieving this method is to stay aware and conscious that you're dreaming while you're dreaming....

To project consciously, the first thing you will want to do is become completely aware that your physical body is asleep while your non-physical body is still awake. This is similar to how lucid dreaming works. Once you feel completely comfortable, exit your physical body and travel into an astral plane environment that seems interesting enough for you....

It's possible to project on command. If this is of interest to you, then there are several methods available for achieving success....The first step in achieving this method is to stay aware and conscious that you're awake while your physical body is asleep. This allows you to take control of your dreams and manipulate them as needed....

There are many different techniques for projecting from the physical body into other dimensions. Which technique works best depends on you and what environment you choose to explore. The best way to achieve success is through practice, time and patience....

Astral Projection: Tips for Mastering Your Skills

For centuries people have explored different methods for projecting their consciousness into the astral plane and back into their physical bodies. It's a highly debated topic within the metaphysical community. Upon researching, there are many different methods used to achieve projection. Each and every technique has their own advantages and disadvantages in order to achieve success....

Although many techniques for astral projection exist, there are a few that are typically considered to be the most powerful. The first method is known as sleep projection.

To enter the dream state from a conscious perspective, stay aware that you're dreaming while you're dreaming. This allows you to take control of your dreams and manipulate them as needed....

Each and every technique has their own advantages and disadvantages in order to achieve success....There is no one right way to go about astral projection. You may have to experiment with multiple techniques before you find one that works best for you....

The next step in achieving a successful projection is learning how to project your consciousness from a conscious perspective into a separate dimension....

Most people in the metaphysical community look at projection as the most difficult part of astral travel. It's not uncommon for people attempting to project their consciousness to feel emotionally overwhelmed, frustrated or simply lost during the process.....

As you gain more experience with astral projection, you will begin to realize that you can actually learn how to consciously project from your physical body. This method is similar to learning a new sport: first off, you do not know how to do it correctly until you actually learn how to do it....

ASTRAL PROJECT TECHNIQUES FOR BEGINNERS AND ADVANCED

These techniques have the potential to allow a person to leave their body and project their consciousness into another space, such as a spiritual realm.

To start your journey, you'll need to start by identifying the issue that is causing the block. For example: You're writing a novel about a character who has an unfortunate addiction, and is still trying to recover from it.

"What is the worst thing I can do to this character?"

This will help you unlock the most creative aspect of your subconscious mind. You can then use this technique in some way to make a powerful main character. You will be able to delve into his or her psyche more deeply than ever before, and write the story like you have never written before.

Another way of using this technique is by getting a general idea of what your novel or short story is about, but putting it down on paper in a stream-of-consciousness manner. The words will flow naturally, and you may find that you get deeper insights into your characters and their actions as well as your plot.

With this technique, you'll also be able to use your own experiences in life as inspiration for the characters and stories.

For example: If you're currently going through a breakup, the emotional turmoil could be used as a way to create depth and complexity in your novels.

"How can I delve deeper inside myself?"

This is a practice that has been around for thousands of years. It helps dissipate all negative thoughts in your mind and allows you to go into a meditative state by emptying your mind completely of all external distractions.

There are many methods to meditate, and you can experiment with them until you find the one that works best for you.

One technique that I personally use, is called "meditation-mimic". This method requires having a recording device such as a digital timer or alarm on your computer so that you can turn it on whenever you need to go into a meditative state.

A study done by Dr. Bruce Greyson, who is a psychiatrist and professor of clinical and forensic psychology at the University of Virginia, suggests that our minds are somehow connected to one another.

Dr. Greyson spent 22 years searching for evidence of what he called the "collective unconscious". This is an area in which all people share in common, and is made up of both our conscious and subconscious minds. Through this process, Dr. Greyson discovered several hints that seem to indicate the existence of this area on our brain. He also discovered that people's experiences can be affected by things they have never encountered before themselves or even known about beforehand.

"How can I find the right mood-setting music?"

Music can change the mood of a scene in an instant. If you're writing a horror story, try putting on some spooky background music to help set the tone for your tale. If you're trying to write a love scene, put on some romantic music or play classical music softly in the background to get the right mood for romance and passion in your novel.

You can also visit your local library and ask them if they have any playlists that go along with certain genres of books.

"How can I get my character's voice to come out naturally?"

If you're having trouble writing your character's dialogue, make sure you ask yourself these questions first: "What is your character thinking at this point?" or "What does this character feel about this situation?" By answering these questions, it will help you assume your character's voice and get the right words to come out naturally on paper.

HOW TO RETURN TO PHYSICAL BODY

1) Think of this as a game. Your goal is to find a special spot where you always see yourself in your third eye. A place where you feel like "you". It might be close to your house or by the beach, for example. You just need to remember that place that makes you feel good when thinking about it.

2) Once you found this special place, align yourself with this place and focus on the middle of your forehead. Then visualize yourself fully entering this spot and feel like you are now there.

3) Now, while you are in this special "you" point (middle of your forehead), focus on your physical body and feel that you have been permanently returning to it since you left it. Keep doing that for a few minutes then move on to the next step.

4) Imagine that you are looking at yourself from the outside as if standing inside a huge mirror. Don't worry about how the appearance looks like, just imagine it in black and white.

5) Now, you need to shift your awareness to a different direction, in such a way that you are looking at yourself from the outside but this time as a bird or other animal, or even another human being. The idea is that you are able to observe yourself from the outside as if you were watching yourself doing some kind of trivial activity or action.

6) Finally, go back to step 2 and try to create some kind of invisible "link" between your physical body and your astral body while you are still looking at yourself from the outside as if in an ordinary mirror. You might feel that you are not in the astral anymore. It's interesting that it feels like you are still in your physical body.

7) After doing this two times, you should be able to move with your astral body from one location to another, and also be able to do some kind of 'physical activity' in your astral body. In other words, once you will have succeed in linking your physical body with your astral one again through this invisible link, it will start affecting the physical one as if it was happening right now.

8) Keep repeating steps 2 - 7 until you can successfully move yourself around the house and do various physical activities without any problems or limitations.

9) After you have mastered the technique, you might want to try to leave your physical body while in the middle of physical activity such as eating or watching TV, but always remember to use these steps 1-8!

10) Once you can leave your physical body and begin physical activities in your astral body without any complications or limitations, you should be able to leave it whenever you want. Start with simple movements like breathing, yawning, movement of your eyes or hands and then proceed slowly while repeating the process until it becomes second nature and automatic.

11) Once you are used to it, try to teleport yourself from one place to another. At first, it might be difficult if you do it too fast and forget about the steps 1-8. Don't worry about it. The idea is that you are able to repeat this process without any effort at all.

12) Once you have mastered the technique of teleportation astral projection, you might want to try doing something more important such as visiting places that are either far away or dangerous or even other planes.

13) The trick for this is to use the same principles but be in a different frequency than your physical one. In other words, while you're on the astral plane, think of the location that you are trying to reach (a place that you might have to pass through) as if it was already passed and at the same time as if it's close. Once you will reach this destination, focus on your physical body and teleport away from there!

14) If things go wrong or suddenly aren't going as expected, just use step 1-8 again and shift yourself back to your physical body quickly! You won't be able to do anything else in your astral body anyway until you return there.

15) If you feel like you are about to fall asleep, just remember that if you stay there too long without returning to your physical body, it might be very dangerous and even fatal. So, whenever you start feeling sleepy while visiting other places as in step 12 or doing new things in your astral body, get back to your physical one as soon as possible.

16) When you feel like it's safe for you to do so, try visiting other planes and near death places. This will be very interesting but also very scary at the same time!

17) It's a good idea not to use these techniques too often or too long. Do some experiments with them first and don't overdo it. You might get tired of the whole process and not want to try anymore. Also, don't use this technique when you're stressed or depressed.

18) By using this passage technique, you will be able to go to any spot in the world without a physical body's limitations. Some techniques might be more powerful than others, but all of them should have the same focus: SOMETHING THAT MAKES YOU FEEL GOOD!!!

19) Once you are able to project with full control and full freedom, it's time for another final step. Think about your goal for this technique. Is it to heal yourself or another human being? Is it to further your knowledge about higher spiritual matters and powers?

20) Now, find a new spot that makes you feel good. It can be a far away place or simply a place in your house that you like more than others. Use the same procedure of steps 1-8. The purpose of this is to connect your astral body with the place and make it feel familiar to you.

21) Once this is done, try leaving your physical body while being in the middle of some activity, such as eating or driving a car for example... and go to that place in your astral body.

Once you're there, shift yourself back to your physical body and continue with the activity as if nothing happened.

22) When you feel more comfortable with this process, try doing all of it without physically leaving your physical body. You can practice this during sleeping time.

23) Once you have succeeded in doing this, try to communicate with some people or beings that are living in that place as if they were physical beings from the other side of the globe! It will be very interesting for many people but they might not be so happy about it at first! If they want to contact you back, don't let them do it until you are sure they are good and kind. They might not be what they seem to be!

24) I hope you enjoyed this technique and that you have learned something new from it.

25) Always remember to stay in a good mood while doing this. If you are unhappy or stressed, it will have an influence on your success rates. So, try using these techniques when you feel like there is nothing else to lose and that this will make you happy or at least happier than before. This will help the process a lot!

26) Now, go ahead and use these techniques in order to achieve the best results for yourself. What works for someone else might not work for you because everything is different! Try different things until you see something working properly.

27) If you want, let me know what's going on in your life. I would love to hear from you!

28) In the meantime, if you've enjoyed this passage technique and found it helpful for yourself or anyone else, I would appreciate if you can share it with anyone else that might find it useful as well.

ASTRAL TRAVEL

Astral travel can be defined as being able to leave your physical body and enter an astral body, or spirit. Astral projection is the ability to travel out of your physical body while dreaming, during meditation, or during lucid dreaming. This can allow you to project your consciousness into different realms such as the dream realm or even another dimension.

Before you attempt to learn how to astral project, there are a few things you should know first. One of the most common mistakes that novice astral projectors make is attempting to do so too early in the morning, or while they are in waking consciousness. It is best to wait until you are experiencing sleep paralysis or are in a dream state. It takes diligent practice to master astral projection, and it will not come easy.

A few signs that show you may be ready to astral project are the ability to have out of body experiences, lucid dreams, and experiences in hypnagogia. One of the most common ways to induce astral projection is through sleep paralysis. When you experience sleep paralysis, your brain activity is similar to when you are dreaming. The most important skill you will need to astral project is breath control. Through breath control, you will learn to manipulate your consciousness and direct it into other worlds.

Based on various reports, there are several methods that have been found to be effective in inducing astral projection. Some of these methods include meditation, lucid dreaming, sleep paralysis, fasting, lucid dreaming exercises, and more.

In order for you to astral project successfully, you will need a quiet place where you can go and relax. This will help eliminate any distraction that could prevent you from achieving it. Astral projection is very similar to lucid dreaming, but I believe it should be approached with the same level of respect as meditation. Astral travel can have lasting effects on your psyche and may even cause some temporary anxiety upon returning to your physical body. Meditation before attempting astral projection, or any altered states of consciousness may help you achieve it more easily.

When you are ready to start attempting astral travel, here is a list of guidelines you should follow:

1. Do not try to astral project at the same time as you attempt lucid dreaming.

2. Before attempting astral projection, set a time limit for yourself. An example of this would be to try to have it occur within 30 seconds after you fall asleep or before your alarm goes off in the morning.

3. It is strongly advised that you choose a quiet place to relax and meditate before attempting astral projection.

4. It is equally important that you have a quiet place where you can rest your physical body.

5. In your mind's eye, imagine yourself in a safe place before attempting to astral project.

6. Relax your body, and consciously try to fall asleep or enter the hypnagogia state of mind.

7. When you feel comfortable and ready, start focusing on your breathing to prevent you from breathing too quickly or too shallowly.

8. Focus on your breathing and try to relax your body.

9. When you are ready, imagine that you are floating up into the air, and then astral project out of your physical body.

10. You should also consider experiencing astral projection while in sleep paralysis as another form of practicing astral travel before attempting to do so during the day, or at night while lucid dreaming.

11. Control your breathing and focus on your surroundings while astral traveling.

12. Try to have as much of a "mind's eye" experience into the astral world as you can, especially if you are attempting it for the first time.

13. Astral projection is most successful when it is done during a lucid dream or during a deep state of hypnagogia where you are not feeling sleepy.

When you successfully astral project, you should feel fine upon returning to your physical body. You might even feel invigorated and refreshed. You should feel fine after astral projection, although it is possible to experience a few side effects such as mild nausea, fatigue, or mild dizziness.

It takes a lot of patience and practice to be able to astral project successfully. It will not happen overnight for most people who are trying to learn how to do it. Astral projection can be a very enlightening experience that has many benefits for your personal growth and spiritual development.

OBEINTRODUCTION

The OBE is often referred to as the near-death experience. It was first coined by Raymond Moody, who has authored a number of books on the subject and has interviewed over 500 people who have had OBEs. While there is not a systematic way to interpret what an OBE feels like, many people describe it as being out of their body but still able to see themselves and feel connected to their physical body in some way. They are often accompanied by vivid memories from past lives or even with contact with mystical beings. The most common setting for an OBE is when the person is either dying or close to death, but they can also occur during sleep, dreams or meditation.

In his book "Life after Life", Moody describes the OBE by laying out all of the things that people have experienced during their OBE. He divides them into three major categories:

The literature review of the subject shows that people have reported a range of experiences. The most common ones can be categorized into three main groups:

Research has shown that those who report having an OBE tend to have different beliefs than those who don't. Those with an OBE are more likely to believe in paranormal phenomena, or at least admit to being open minded to it, than those who do not report seeing a double during near death experiences.

Several surveys have been performed that show the beliefs of people who have experienced an OBE. One of these studies, which was performed in the United Kingdom, showed that out of 746 people who had an OBE, 85% believed in life after death. In another study done by Janice Holden she found that in a group of people who had an NDE, 74.4% said they believed in life after death while only 35% of those who survived but did not have an NDE believed in it and 7.6% did not believe but were open to the reality. Yet another study found that those who reported an NDE were more likely to believe in life after death than those who didn't have a near-death experience.

There has not been any studies that state the percentage of people who have had an NDE or OBE and then later on convert to a religion such as Christianity, Islam, Hinduism and Buddhism but some people who feel they have had contact with supernatural being during an NDE might turn towards religion as a result. That said, there are some surveys where researchers asked if the person was religious before their experience and what their beliefs are now. One study showed that 29% of people surveyed were previously religious pre-NDE and 64% became more religious post-NDE.

In his book "The Celestine Prophecy", James Redfield describes an OBE where he sees himself the night before he dies. However, in a letter to the editor, Redfield states that this experience was in fact not an OBE but a dream he had after suffering a heart attack. Studies also show that some NDE survivors have reported having dreams after their NDE and some have been able to recall the details of the dreams later on, although this is not the case with all people who have NDEs.

There has not been any official studies done on people who claim to have had contact with angels or other mystical beings during an OBE. However, there have been people who have claimed to have seen such a being during an OBE. In his book entitled "Encounter with the Living God: A Book of Answers", Kenneth Ring gives three accounts of people who believe they had contact with angels while they were undergoing an OBE. The first testimony was from a woman named Elizabeth, who describes her encounter with an angel. She stated that she felt as if she were "in a cloud" lying on her bed and although she felt comfortable she could not move or speak. Then she saw someone walking towards the bed and described him as looking like Jesus Christ. He then proceeded to touch her on the forehead and give her a single white rose that she felt a tremendous surge of energy as he did so. After he was finished she could not see him anymore but she felt his presence and continued to feel it after that. She describes feeling warm and happy after this encounter. The second testimony was from Robert, who states that while in his OBE he saw what looked like "the typical depiction of an angel" with wings and halo, very bright white light and nothing else. The only thing he heard was the word "follow" until it stopped being repeated which meant to him that something had happened or someone was finished saying something they had needed to say. He then says that he saw a "V" shaped path where one could go, and he would have liked to follow that. He describes the feeling as extremely powerful and sensitive. The final testimony was for a woman named Carol who is in her mid-forties and shares very similar beliefs to Kenneth Ring. In her account of an experience where she saw an angel she said that she felt like she was being transported from one place to another at great speeds, an incredible wave of pressure hit her causing her to cry out in pain; but then something very soothing happened and she drifted into what seemed like a tunnel. When she came back, she could remember everything that had happened perfectly while in her OBE.

There have been many studies done that attempt to prove that OBEs are in fact hallucinations or night terrors.

One study was conducted by Kenneth Ring and his team. They presented two cases with a total of 18 participants. In one case, a woman named Wendy had a dream that she was having an encounter with her deceased mother who died at age twenty-three, being reborn into another mother's womb prior to birth, and then being born as a baby again. Wendy later reported the dream and wrote down her personal experiences during her OBE after reading about OBEs in her journal. In another case, a woman named Mary had a dream that she was lying in bed and in her dream she saw a man standing at the foot of her bed. She also wrote about this experience in her journal. In both of these cases the researchers found that the people involved seemed to have no previous knowledge about OBEs or NDEs; were unable to distinguish between reality and fantasy prior to their experience and after their experiences were unable to recall any other details beyond those they had recorded. The researchers concluded that these cases suggest that an OBE can be caused by purely psychological means such as dreams, hallucinations or memories from childhood.

In a few cases, people have claimed to have had their NDE and then later on reported seeing a being that looked like Jesus Christ. In some cases, they also would experience another vision after this saying it was Jesus Christ and another being. Intriguingly, these visions later ceased to exist or were replaced with other visions that do not resemble the original vision. In one such case a man named Shawn described the details of his vision in his journal for several months before it disappeared completely; when it did he wrote as if he had never experienced what he saw before. Another example is of a woman named Bernadette who after her NDE experienced other visions that did not resemble what she actually saw during her NDE. However, it was when she later went to a psychologist to have her NDE examined that the OBE visions ceased. The psychologist concluded that her visions were a product of her imagination.

A study was performed by Thomas D. Soal and his team at Stanford University. They conducted interviews with 50 NDE survivors, and then asked them to provide him with stories containing the following phrases: "I felt like I was being lifted into heaven," "I felt as if I were floating in space," "Everything seemed very bright and shining," and "I saw beings who appeared like angels." The researchers then took these stories and came up with an overall description of what each NDE survivor saw during their experience. They found that more than 98% of those interviewed said they saw a being with wings or clothing that looked like a woman; however, they did not find any correlation between the frequency of this phrase in their subjects' descriptions and the type of NDE they experienced.

A study was performed by Christopher J. French at the University of Manchester. The purpose of this study was to gather information about experiences during an OBE where people feel as if they are floating or flying. The researchers interviewed thirteen people who had an experience during their OBE that was described as floating or flying. The participants went on to describe that after they came back they did not have a sense of reality or memory; and once they regained consciousness, all they could remember was what had happened while they were under this other perception. The researcher concludes that these experiences are not simply dreams experienced while sleeping.

OBE DESCRIPTION

OBE stands for Out-of-Body Experience. Out-of-body experiences can happen to most people, at least once in their lives. People who have had an OBE usually describe themselves gaining the ability to look down on their own body from above, where they see a translucent image of their body on the bed below them. In order to get back into your body, you usually need someone else's help - whether it be another person touching you and commanding your attention or simply through some form of voluntary astral projection while sleeping.

The reason why people usually describe themselves as translucent during an OBE is that the astral body is not physical in the same sense as the physical body. It is a projection of your own consciousness that travels outside of your physical embodiment, which is why you are able to travel to other places and see what people are doing there - you can spy on them without being detected yourself.

Within my own out-of-body experiences, I never saw myself as translucent but rather as a shadow shade or black mist. The out-of-body experience happened when I was in my early teens. I was sitting in a chair and dozed off. As I closed my eyes, I felt myself flying up through the ceiling and out into the night sky. It was incredibly exciting for me to be able to look down on my own house, all lit up underneath me. Then, suddenly I flew what seemed like miles away from home and over a city that looked like it had been taken out of a futuristic movie - it was all lit up with huge bright lights everywhere and huge buildings towering over everything else. Right then, as I was looking at it, the entire city just looked like it blew up - there were fireballs raining down everywhere on everything. It was scary seeing everything blow up like that, but I just kept staring at it. Then it was over.

Another time that I remember having an out-of-body experience was when I was sleeping. It must have been around noon at this time and I had been sleeping all morning with my girlfriend (who has now become my wife), but then she got up first because she had to wake up early to go into work that day. I tried to fight her off because I wasn't ready to get out of bed yet, but she just kept tugging at me. She was still half asleep and I'm not sure how she knew something had happened but something had definitely woken her up. "You were having a dream about running and you were kicking the covers off the bed," she said, shaking me awake. I sat up in the bed and shook myself awake. After that, when I started to fall asleep again, I could see myself getting sucked through a long dark tunnel that was going down all the way into the darkness below the earth. It made me feel uneasy because I couldn't tell where it would end or if there would be anything scary waiting for me there. It was a really scary feeling, but then I was suddenly brought back into my body. I woke up to my girlfriend shaking me again. She told me that I had been talking aloud in my sleep and she heard me say something about being scared of the tunnel. It felt very alien and surreal to experience something like this while sleeping, since it felt like I had never left my body, even though I was definitely awake at the time when it happened.

I have had numerous astral projection experiences in my life, and I've always been able to have them at will. I can start and stop them whenever I want, which is a great feeling of independence and power when you can go on an astral trip whenever you want to, or not at all. I started having out-of-body experiences back in the early 1990s when I was into doing a lot of drugs - both hard drugs like acid and pot as well as psychedelic hallucinogens like DMT. Even though I was also into lucid dreaming, I'm still not sure if it was the drugs that caused my OBEs or if they were always there but just never triggered before.

In order to have out-of-body experiences, you need to be in a state of relaxation - almost all of them happen asleep. You should have your mind and body relaxed to the point where you are not too aware of external stimuli, but also not too relaxed where you are falling asleep - you want to be somewhere in between there. You also need to be able to relax your physical body and let go of all mental thoughts and worries so you can drift off into sleep. You can do this by doing meditation, taking a bath, walking through the woods or even doing some light exercise before going to bed. The best way to ease into the process is just to sit quietly until you start feeling sleepy - it doesn't really matter in what position you're sitting as long as you're not being held down by something (like a sudden need to use the bathroom). It's important that you do not keep trying to go back up into your higher self until you feel completely relaxed in order for it to work right. Usually, this means that you're already feeling drowsy and are starting to slip off into sleep. This is not so much of a problem for longer OBEs like those that induce sleep paralysis, but is important to keep in mind for shorter OBEs that involve just going out of your body while fully conscious and stay in the higher self.

In order to successfully achieve an out-of-body experience, it's a good idea to read up about how astral projection is achieved and then try different methods until you find what works for you. I have read several books about the subject and have tried multiple techniques to achieve OBEs; I like to imagine myself as a superhero with various kinds of abilities such as energy projection, astral projection and many others. For example, I can project myself into other people's dreams by simply thinking about them during the day and when I do this, they will most likely seem to be conscious during their dream - it may even be possible for me to communicate with them in their dreams just by thinking about them. I can also project myself into other people's bodies, like that of a family member or a friend, and look at the same place with their eyes. I've done this on many occasions and it is great fun seeing things through other people's eyes. It gets really wild when I attempt to do this with somebody who has never had an out-of-body experience before and they will always be completely confused as to why they are seeing things differently now. One time I projected myself into my sister's body and she started saying that there was something in her head - she felt like there was somebody else inside there with her! This has happened several times and it is just so awesome.

BEST TECHNIQUES OF ASTRAL PROJECT

There are lots of people who wish to know about astral travel techniques but for some reason they never really seem to get any information.

Astral travel is the process of separating ones consciousness from their physical body to enable them to explore the universe, look for answers or solve a problem

Many people have used this type of out-of-body experience as a form of spiritual enlightenment, personal development or even looking for adventure. No matter your intention it is important that you learn how to safely venture into these realms...

Different people will have different experiences, the nicest thing about astral projection is that it can be experienced by just about anyone provided they can distract themselves from their current physical body.

If you don't get what you want, accept it and move on.

-Richard Bach

Achieving a successful Out Of Body Experience depends on several factors...

Best Astral Projection - Techniques for Out of Body Experiences

The simplest way to achieve an OBE is to simply relax your body so that it begins floating away from your physical form as if your consciousness was being pulled upward by a magnet.

You can also achieve this state by laying or sitting down and imagining that your body is made out of helium and floating up into the air. This is often done through visualization. Another way to do it is to stay calm and breathe slowly, imagine that you are getting some kind of sensation (like if a balloon was tied around your fingers or something), any sort of sensation, then it might pull your consciousness out with the sensation.

This is a fundamental technique but it is still a beginner's technique that requires practice and patience. Among the various techniques listed below there are more complex techniques to achieve an OBE.

Out of body experience the classic out of body experience involves having your consciousness leave your body while you are sleeping or resting and entering another location. Since your physical body is not moving, you can fly around the room or even the house - or even outside to places further away.

Possible as it might be, Astral Projection, often referred to as astral travel or astral projection is usually not advisable because of negative consequences associated with such an experience. It should therefore be considered a dangerous practice, especially if you have no prior experience.

However strong the interest, some people still find it hard to astral project. Some doubt their ability to do it or are scared of the experience.

For those who really want to have that experience of Astral Projection, there can be several causes for their failure –not being relaxed enough when attempting a projection, lack of motivation due to your false belief that it is impossible, or even not knowing how to get started.

To avoid these problems, always ensure that you have realistic expectations –you must be ready with a positive mindset and proper preparation before starting on your astral journey. The easiest way to get started is actually through relaxation exercises.

Awareness is the best way to control your mind and body.

When you relax, you become aware of everything that happens around you. When proposing techniques, for example, you can see everything that happens around you and also know what will happen in advance.

You can be aware of all your sensations even if you are lying down with closed eyes. You may notice sounds that someone makes when walking across the room or feel the bed shaking when someone walks past it. All these things help distract from your physical body so that it gets into a state where it can leave easily.

Since you are aware of everything, you can focus your mind on one thing and be aware of that when something else happens.

The best way to become aware of your surroundings is through visualization. Always imagine yourself leaving your physical body. What does it feel like? What does the room look like? Who's around you? How are they reacting? Before you start at least have a basic grasp of what people look and sound like as they move around the house or in everyday situations.

You'll find that with a little imagination and a willingness to turn off certain thoughts, even the most mundane experiences can become exciting or even breathtaking. Keep it up and you will be well on your way to astral projection.

This could either be a particular sensation in your body or a sensation that is not coming from within you. All the while, keep reminding yourself that you want to experience Astral Projection.

What I usually do is I imagine myself in a dark room with no doors or windows at all. By doing this, I find myself slipping out of my body very easily (though I am not sure if this will work for everyone).

Colorful Rainbows

Another method is to imagine a colorful rainbow as a tunnel. You are the center of it. Go into the center and you will find yourself in another dimension.

A Quick Note on Astral Projection

Our bodies are constantly producing electrical impulses and when we fall asleep, these impulses are still there, but our minds aren't aware of them anymore so it creates an entirely different experience. This is how hypnosis works...

This happens with astral projection too where your mind is willing to stay conscious but your body isn't so it just floats away and you start to experience places that aren't really there ... It's not too hard to achieve if you know what you're doing.

Invisible World

A trip to the invisible world is the next step after astral projection. It is a place where you can travel in your astral body (your mind) and not your physical body. You may find yourself in other times, places, or even in other dimensions. Your consciousness will still be conscious of the physical reality around you but your physical body will have no concept of the things that lie beyond you.

It's a lot like having the power to teleport whenever you want. You are able to move through walls, ceilings and floors so long as there's nothing blocking them.

You are still stuck within this world though –if you try to go beyond it, you'll find yourself back at your location.

What's The Best Way To Have An Out Of Body Experience?

There are a wide variety of OBE techniques that you can do to have an out of body experience. Some are simpler than others, and some require more work and determination to achieve. However there is a wide variety available to suit your individual needs.

Some Techniques to Achieve an OBE

The following are some techniques which I have used successfully in my personal search for astral projection. They have worked for me and they will probably work for you as well but don't expect them to work overnight. These techniques take time and practice but once you get the hang of it, it will be second nature for you.

Cognitive Sweep

This involves clearing your mind with meditation. You need to clear your mind of all thoughts and worries and keep reminding yourself that you want to have an out of body experience. Once you've gotten rid of any thoughts in your mind, let them come back only when it is time to sleep.

By doing this, your conscious mind will be in the right state and it will be easier for you to slip into a trance-like state that is perfect for astral projection. This will also initiate a specific response from the unconscious part of your mind which will make this possible for you.

Before going to bed, visualize yourself being able to project yourself from within your physical body.

Keep reminding yourself that you want to have an out of body experience. This should make it much easier for you.

You may even find yourself having this kind of experience during sleep…

Dreaming

You might find that sometimes while you are dreaming, you actually become conscious of yourself and what is around you. If that happens, just try to stay there for a while and see what happens. Soon your dream will center on something else and you can get back into the dream properly.

MANY MORE TECHNIQUES TO TRY

For those who want to explore the out-of-body state, there are many techniques and practices to try. Astral projection is a subtle phenomenon which can be difficult if methods are not understood.

Step 1: Grounding technique for astral projection

Grounding is a popular technique used by many introverts and sensory sensitive individuals as well as those with neurological disorders such as migraines. The idea is that grounding oneself before an attempt at astral projection reduces the risk of encountering further episodes of psychosis or hallucinations due to mental trauma from sensory overload stemming from an encounter with an out-of-body experience.

Grounding can be accomplished by the simple act of holding on to any nearby fixed object, rock, tree or the floor. It is important to get comfortable and relaxed before attempting astral projection.

The following steps will help you to become familiar with grounding techniques:

1) **Position yourself in a comfortable chair or bed.**

2) **Bring each hand up to a point on your body where there is no contact between your hands and body, but feel the**

contact between your palms and the surface they are touching; this is known as a fingertip-touchpoint connection.

3) Next, move your hands to a point on your body where there is no contact between your hands and body; this is known as an arm-length connection.

4) Now move back to the fingertip-touchpoint connection. You will feel very relaxed at this point.

5) Inhale deeply and exhale all the air out of your lungs to feel a sense of calmness and relaxation.

6) Inhale again deeply, but this time keep the air in your lungs. Think about things you're grateful for as you exhale slowly.

7) Inhale again, but this time hold your breath a bit longer than before.

8) Now grasp something firmly using both hands. This will help you to recover from any dizziness or disorientation you may be experiencing as you begin to project out of your body.

9) Keep holding on to that object and breathe deeply again, similar to step 6 above.

10) At this point, if you have not already had an out-of-body experience, the process may take about 30 seconds. You will want to take slow, deep breaths and keep reading.

11) Keep holding on to that object and breathing deeply. You will soon feel vibrations in your body and may even hear vibrations, too.

12) Next you may begin to feel a slight tingling sensation in your hands as you hold on to the object. This will go away after about 10 seconds; this is the beginning of a separation from your physical body.

13) Next you may find it difficult to breathe naturally; this is normal during astral projection, and you should keep breathing deeply just like in step 6 above.

14) Now just let go of the object that you have been holding on to.

15) You will begin to float out of your body.

16) At this point, you may feel a little dizzy or disoriented; this is normal so just keep breathing deeply until it passes or if it does not pass, try the grounding exercise again. You may also feel as though you are attached to something solid, even after you have let go of the grounding object. I am not attached to my physical body. I am only a projection. I am not attached to my physical body."

17) Now that you are floating, you will notice stars or different things passing by you in the distance. They will seem to be close, but after a short while they will move farther away from you and eventually fade into oblivion.

18) There is no need to try and follow whatever was moving; just breathe slowly and comfortably as though you are out for a nice walk on a beautiful night in the country.

19) You will be able to stay in the astral world for quite a long time. You should not be worried if you cannot hear anything or if your surroundings seem to fade into nothingness around you.

20) Shield yourself with love, consciously accepting that everything that is arising in this experience is a gift from the Universe carrying its vibration of Divine Love, with which you can live consciously moving through this life as intended.

21) The astral projection technique described above can be used with all other techniques mentioned on this site and it can also be used when not undertaking an astral project at all.

Step 2: Visualization techniques for astral projection

Astral projection can be a very confusing, scary and disorienting experience. Through the power of imagination, we can see what our spirit guides and angels look like, as well as other beings that may be involved in the project. The strength of your imagination affects how you project; so before you attempt to astral project, it helps to know what it looks like. It's easier to astral project if you imagine yourself in a beautiful location and see yourself looking into the eyes of an angelic being. If you have an out-of-body experience, visualization is the companion technique you will likely use to do so.

The techniques below are tools that can be used to successfully project out of your physical body into the astral plane. Astral projection can be a very pleasant and magical experience if it is done the right way. So please use these techniques correctly and, as always, pray for guidance when attempting a projection.

Astral Projection Technique #1: ColorVisualization Technique

Visualizing in colorful light is, in many ways, a shortcut to astral projection. However, many people who have tried this technique have not had a full-blown projection experience. The reason for this is that you still need to practice the "grounding technique" outlined above. It is recommended that you do a grounding exercise at least three times before attempting an astral projection with this technique.

Here's how to use the ColorVisualization Technique:

First, prepare yourself to astral project. Grounding exercises should be done three times and visualization techniques should be engaged several times per day at first, in order for your subconscious mind to learn how to visualize projections well. Next, start by relaxing yourself as much as possible. If you tend to be tense, take 5 – 10 minutes to meditate. If you do not have any meditation experience, try the simple relaxation technique below.

Step 1: Sit in a comfortable position and close your eyes, notice that your body is relaxed. Now force yourself to relax further and imagine yourself floating at the top of the page above your body. You will look at something far away and move slowly towards it. Tune out all thoughts and feelings from your mind except for images of that faraway thing you are moving towards and relax even more. Now picture a beautiful color such as blue, which is important because colors have energy. Focus on the blue energy and try to imagine it moving towards you. It is important that you feel it moving towards you. If the energy is not moving towards you, imagine that you are seeing it move toward your face. Also, try imagining that this energy has a glowing quality to it. The more vivid your imagination, the easier this technique will be for you. If this does not work at first try just closing your eyes for a few seconds before opening them again and continue with the visualization process. If you find yourself getting distracted, just close your eyes again and continue. Try to imagine the color of blue reaching towards you until it touches your face and you have a realization that the color has wrapped around your face. When this happens, open your eyes slowly and stare at the ceiling for a moment as though you are trying to figure out what is happening to you. You will probably feel lightheaded as well as some nausea, which is perfectly normal – it is caused by the body releasing endorphins after being startled by an imaginary event that occurred in your brain.

Step 2: Immediately after opening your eyes, do three grounding exercises. (The grounding exercises are to be performed after each visualization session that you do.) First, stand up and notice how your feet feel. Next, walk around a little bit and pay attention to how your body feels. Finally, clasp your hands behind your back and try to feel the vertebrae in your neck.

Visualization Technique #2: Polarity Visualization

Before you can master projection techniques, it is important to know what the astral plane feels like. The following technique allows you to become familiar with this feeling:

Again, make sure that you are thoroughly grounded before beginning this exercise and ensure that you have performed at least 3 grounding exercises before attempting polarity visualization. It is best to perform this on a full moon night if you can. Begin by relaxing yourself as much as you can. If you need to, begin with some simple meditation techniques. After about 5 minutes of relaxed breathing, close your eyes and imagine a glowing orb of white light appearing in front of your face, about two feet away. The light will not be blinding but instead will be just bright enough that you cannot look at it for too long without averting your eyes. Shape the light of white light into a sword by holding it in your right hand and feeling the nape of your neck with the tip of that same hand. The sword should be approximately as long as your arm, so that you can keep it pointed straight out in front of you, between your eyes and shoulder. Feel the energy from this sword flowing down to its tip at your nape. When you feel ready, raise this sword up so that its end is pressing against the top of your head and allow this energy to course through you and go down into the ground where it connects to source.

COMPARISON OBE/ASTRAL PROJECTION /ASTRAL TRAVEL

Out of Body Experiences (OBE), astral projection, and astral travel have often been used interchangeably. These three terms have been used to define a variety of experiences involving the separation of one's consciousness from their body.

Astral projection and astral travel both refer to a process of consciously leaving the body in an out-of-body experience. In contrast, OBEs often involve leaving the body involuntarily during sleep or fainting. In many cases, a projection is done with full conscious awareness while an OBE is not. However, there is overlap between these experiences with some people describing the separation of their consciousness as "floating above my body."

Furthermore, most astral projections entail travelling to other non-physical locations that can be reached through conscious thought or meditation. Astral travel is usually done without the use of a vehicle, such as a spaceship.

In contrast, OBEs are usually associated with the experience of moving through a narrow tunnel towards the light. This is coupled with recalling one's physical body while out of it.

These experiences can happen simultaneously and therefore lead to even more confusion when trying to differentiate between the phenomena. While these experiences do share some commonalities, there are several differences that make clear distinctions between them.

The first major difference between these three experiences involves the bodily location of the projection or travel. OBEs occur within the physical realm, but a projection and travel occur outside of it. These are not to be confused with near-death experiences that sometimes involve physically leaving one's body.

The second major difference between these three involves the location traveled to during the experience. In OBEs, people typically travel to non-physical locations such as heaven or parallel dimensions. In contrast, most projections and travels lead people to other physical locations that may or may not exist on Earth. Specifically, they are usually higher-dimensional realms that are less dense than our physical world.

Another difference between the three lies in the experiences of those who have undergone them. At their most basic level, people who experience an OBE do not remember their trip outside of their body while people who experience a projection or travel usually do. However, this is not always the case. This may lead to the realization that these experiences may be similar in different ways.

A projection can involve a person remembering leaving their body behind and traveling to other realms. A person may also experience an OBE while astral travelling. In these cases, they are sometimes able to recall their travels or experiences outside of their body during a projection or travel respectively due to emerging from another state of consciousness than was present when they left their physical body behind.

There is also the possibility of a person experiencing a projection while unconscious and dreaming. This is called lucid dreaming and can occur when people are mentally awake but still asleep. In these cases, people can be fully conscious during an experience such as astral projection and travel occurring within their dreams.

Many people who experience projections or travel are often frightened by them and many try to escape from them through closing their eyes or other means. However, there are some who are able to control what happens in these experiences through their thoughts while others may not be able to control it at all. This can lead to even more variations in these experiences for people who have had them.

Astral projection is a phenomenon where a spirit or mind separates from the physical body and travels into the astral plane, as well as other dimensions that may exist in this universe. This may also be referred to as astral travel, soul travel or remote viewing. In most cases, this is done without taking any physical vehicles, like an airplane. The second definition of astral projection states that there is the existence of an alternate body separate from the physical body.

In most cases, people can project their consciousness outside of their body without traveling anywhere. This is a similar phenomenon to lucid dreaming or spiritual journeying. Some cases involve travelling to other physical locations on Earth while others do not. However, some people do realize they are projecting and are able to control it consciously with the use of tools like magic and witchcraft.

In most cases, the term astral projection refers to the experience of a person leaving their physical body while asleep. Some people refer to this as an OBE or out-of-body experience since this is usually done without taking any physical vehicles. However, most people use the terms "Astral Projection" and "OBE" interchangeably when trying to describe an experience which describes the same phenomenon. In both cases, there is a separation of consciousness from the physical body and may involve travelling through non-physical realms.

To some people, travelling beyond the physical world is possible because of the existence of an alternate body to the physical body that is separate from it. This is known as astral projection or out-of-body experience and refers to the experience a person has when leaving their physical body while asleep. In most cases, this happens when there are two different states of consciousness besides being awake or asleep. The first is known as lucid dreaming where a person becomes consciously aware that they are dreaming while asleep. The second involves leaving one's body while remaining conscious at all times in what is known as astral projection or OBE.

Astral projection can occur during sleeping, meditation, lucid dreaming and advanced hypnotic states. It is also possible to have a person's awareness of their physical body take control and project themselves out of their physical body temporarily.

Most people who experience this separation of consciousness from their physical body are not aware that they have done so, but those who do often become frightened by it or try to find a way back inside. Some people are able to separate from the physical world on purpose via hypnosis. Some also use magic for the same purpose sometimes. This is often done while asleep by many traditions, including meditation, lucid dreaming and shamanic techniques. Some people also use other means, such as astral projection devices to induce an out-of-body experience.

In some cases, a person is able to manipulate their consciousness and travel out of their body while being conscious of it. This may mean being aware of where they are going or being able to remotely view a physical location. In this case, the person projecting their consciousness is consciously projecting themselves into a different location in their mind. They are often unaware that this is happening while it occurs and do not remember anything about the experience when it is over aside from some vague memories.

Some people are also able to control where they go during this out-of-body experience, while others may be completely unaware of the process.

Astral Projection Devices

Astral Projection Machines

The astral projection machines are devices that are specifically designed for the purpose of achieving an out-of-body experience. They include a variety of different ways to induce an OBE and provide a variety of functions for all kinds of purposes. It's usually recommended that everyone should start from learning how to do it on their own first, before using such devices. These machines can work with the use of their specific features in achieving an OBE.

There are believed to be multiple ways of inducing out-of-body experiences, which include but not limited to lucid dreaming, astral projection and hypnagogia. These methods are often believed to be the easiest ones for inducing an OBE. Using these techniques, it is possible for those who have difficulty in achieving a conscious separation of their consciousness from their physical bodies. Some people may even achieve an OBE without knowing how or trying at all.

While the traditional notion of astral projections involves travelling beyond physical locations while awake, there have been cases where an individual travels through non-physical realms while being unconscious or asleep at the time. This occurs when the person is dreaming while remaining unconscious.

There are also documented cases where people have very realistic dreams of flying or floating in the air, only to wake up and realize that they were actually physically moving around their room during the time of their dream. This is known as sleepwalking and is associated with a type of night terrors known as sleepwalking. There are also many documented cases where people have claimed that they have been able to project their consciousness out of their bodies while asleep but no evidence to support this has been found.

Whether the dreams of flying, floating or travelling through non-physical realms that take place while asleep and unaware are true astral projections or just a result of the mind at work is not known for sure. However, there have also been documented cases where people experience lucid dreams in which have been considered as out-of-body experiences during which they were conscious and aware of their physical bodies at all times.

In recent years, various devices have been developed for inducing out-of-body experiences by intending to isolate and stimulate specific parts of the brain. These include synaesthesia which is supposedly triggered by stimulating small regions of the brain with electrical impulses. This can be utilized to trigger the induction of various unusual sensory perceptions that are similar to those which are triggered during an out-of-body experience.

Neurofeedback has also been used and involves reading the electrical activity in the brain, rather than directly stimulating it. In recent years, there have been many studies being conducted on how to mentally induce out of body experiences using both of these techniques and there are still numerous people who believe that this is possible even though research has shown that inducing an out-of-body experience is very difficult.

REGULAR ASTRAL PROJECTIONSAND WHO WANTS TO KNOW MORE OFTHE MECHANICS AND PROBLEMS THAT ARISE DURING THEIR ASTRAL PROJECTIONS

D id you know that a person who can consciously project their astral body while out of their physical body is called an Astral Projector? It's also sometimes referred to as astro-projection or projection, out-of-body experience. It's an incredible sensation and one that many people long for. However, as with any great experience, there are also costs to consider.

Physical Symptoms of Astral Projections

There are some physical symptoms that people associated with Astral Projections; however, there are also other factors that can contribute to these symptoms. Physical problems may arise from poor sleep, lack of time spent healthy like exercising and eating well, stress or anxiety during the day or any other major life events that are taking place in your life. Basically, anything that causes stress and not enough exercise will cause some type of physical issue such as muscle fatigue, back pain, joint aches, eye strain and other general bodily discomfort.

Astral Traveling into High Places

The other major problem associated with Astral Projecting is the potential for falling to certain places. Falling is a big issue and one that must be taken seriously. It's important to keep in mind that the Astral Reaches are higher places, meaning that when you project into those areas, there's really no telling what you can run into or who might be there. Imagine falling out of your projective body and plummeting to the ground below.

Finding Yourself in the Negative

Another major issue associated with Astral Projections is finding yourself in the negative. The Astral realms are places of consciousness and different energies. There are also people living there that cause emotions of fear, anger or any other emotions that you feel during your daily life. If you do a regular projection, it's possible to find yourself somewhere the exact opposite of what you really want to experience. While most people can get around this by avoiding dark places while they're projecting or staying on high grounds, there's another way to avoid this problem and it involves a little self-control and discipline during your projection.

Solving the Problem of Astral Projections and how to Prevent Them

There are a few ways to prevent Astral Projections from becoming a problem. First and foremost would be to know that you can avoid it all together. If you're feeling tired or not getting enough sleep, then you need to make sure that you focus on getting good rest. If you choose to take on more work or pressure during those times instead, it's possible that your body will suffer for it hours later when you go into full projection mode.

Another way to prevent the issue of regular projections would be to take advantage of a program that allows you to lessen and eventually end your Astral Projection Regimes. Astral Projection Regimes, generally, are methods that allow you to experience your Astral Projections safely but with little or no chance of falling. By using these methods, it's possible for you to avoid the issues associated with Astral Projections and live a full and healthy life without having to deal with any of the negative conditions or possible injuries.

There are a number of Astral Projection Regimes that are detailed within this site and these methods allow you to project with ease and have a great time while doing so. One method that you can use is called The Kinesis Method which allows you to gently return to the physical body or explore your consciousness at an even higher level. It's important to note that if you do get hurt during the exercise, there are various ways in which you can avoid the issue of leaving your body before it's too late for you.

The next step in avoiding the possibility of regular Astral Projections would be for people to check out all sessions from our Mind Control Techniques section. These sessions are a great way to help you get a handle on your emotions during the day and before you go to bed. The Mind Control Techniques section also includes guides that you can easily follow in order to gain greater self-control over yourself. As an added benefit, when you have control over yourself, it's easier for you to avoid the issue of falling during your projection and into dangerous circumstances.

The final step would be to learn about how you can reset your physical body and prepare it for sleep. Regular sleep helps individuals access high levels of consciousness without having to actively project their Astral Bodies while they rest. It's important to note that there are a lot of benefits to having regular rest periods. If you're getting the proper amount of sleep during the day, it's easier for you to be more self-aware without feeling like your body needs attention.

LEARN THE PRACTICAL HOW TO OF ASTRAL PROJECTION

These are ways to practice and begin to astral project now. You will learn about: dreams, lucid dreaming, meditation techniques, and supplements for your spiritual work, what makes up the physical body and how it can affect astral projection, what happens on different planes of consciousness during an astral projection and much more!

Astral projection is the act of out-of-body experience (OBE) where a person can project their mind or spirit outside of the body. It's typically accompanied by an OBE where the person has a clear vision of themselves floating above their bodies or sitting in their chair. It's possible for people to have astral projection without an accompanying OBE, but these experiences are usually more common when they do occur. It's similar to lucid dreaming in that a person is conscious as they leave their bodies.

How Does Astral Projection Work?

The scientific definition of OBE explains that it is the projection of the mind outside of the body and into the other side, or another dimension. However, who's to say what exactly "the other side" or "another dimension" is? Personally, I think that's a bunch of BS. There are multiple planes of consciousness (physical, astral, etheric, etc.) and OBEs can occur on any one of these planes depending on what you're doing and where you want to go. For example, if you're getting dressed for work in the morning a person may see themselves waking up in their bed and not out of body like an astral projection.

What Happens When Someone Projects?

Again, this is pretty much different for everyone as everyone's processes are unique to them. People have different ways of dealing with the flood of information that is experienced during an OBE. It's the combination of all these factors that make up a person's experience. The visual details, the distance to other people and objects, the feeling of weightlessness and position in space, and how a person receives information about themselves and their surroundings are all important in determining what happens to a person when they astral project.

Most often, people experience events or happenings from their past lives. Often times these are experiences where they made a mistake or bad decision that left them with some negative repercussions in their lives. On most occasion's people hear voices, see bright lights or images while astral projecting. Some people remember visiting different places, having conversations with people, and experiencing things that they want to manifest in the physical world. These events are called precognitions and are a popular subject for those who are interested in astral projection. Astral projections are typically short lived (around 1–5 minutes) as lying still for extended periods of time can cause the body to shut down or start to decay.

How Do You Astral Project?

The best way to experience astral projection is by using your imagination and doing some mental exercises before bed at night. I also recommend you start your day off with some meditation techniques. Usually in the morning or during the day when you think about doing an astral projection, your mind has already been primed for these types of experiences as it has already started to work. For example, if you're lying in bed just before going to sleep and you close your eyes. This is a time when you're more prone to start hallucinating and having OBEs.

How Do I Experience Astral Projection?

With some training and practice, anyone can astral project. It takes hard work and dedication but it's worth it! Once you begin to experience OBEs on a regular basis, then astral projection becomes something that happens more often by default. For some people, doing astral projection is a way to connect with others who have projected before them. They'll often report hearing other people's voices or feeling the presence of deceased family members who have passed. Astral projection can also help those that suffer from depression to feel less depressed. If you're looking for a better life and want to wake up every day feeling amazing, astral projection is the way to go!

Astral Projection for Beginners – Sleep Like Humans Do

Many cultures around the world have ritualistic sleep patterns that are based on cycles of napping and waking. As we all know, this type of sleep pattern has been lost in Western culture due to industrialization. However, some people still turn to this method to help them get better quality sleep and start experiencing astral projection earlier.

According to author and researcher Graham Hancock, the ancient Egyptians had an elaborate system of astral ritualism that was used for healing and spiritual development. He claims that the ancient Hebrews also practiced a type of astral occultism popularly referred to as Kaballa. This is similar in nature to Egyptian Kemetic science and has existed in one form or another since the dawn of civilization. It was also reported by Jesuit priests who visited Mexico in the 16th century that Aztec people practiced a type of OBE called teotl (God) walking where they would walk through the heavens at night.

If we go back even further in history, the practice of sleeping while wrapped in animal skins was not just a survival technique but also known as a way to induce visions. Native Americans were known for wrapping themselves in buffalo and bear furs during sleep. This was not only to keep warm but also to receive guidance from their higher selves or the spirits around them. And finally, most people have heard of the modern term lucid dreaming where a person is consciously awake while dreaming. The Greeks called these types of dreams noosidēmos (seeing within). In some Eastern cultures this is considered a type of astral projection and is used as a form of escapism and entertainment.

PRACTICAL ADVICE ABOUT HOW TO ASTRAL TRAVEL

For many westerners, astral travel is an ambiguous concept, and is often dismissed as a pseudoscience or taken to be synonymous with out-of-body experiences (OBEs). It's typically seen by the scientific community and many spiritual schools alike as hallucinations, dreams or illusions. However, there are people who have had very real experiences with astral traveling; some even claim to use it for self-exploration or psychotherapy purposes.

It will describe how to establish the principle of astral body separation and provide some information about crossing the astral body threshold and entering the astral plane.

We will begin by investigating what an astral body is; how it works, and what its limitations are in terms of traveling. Finally, we will get into the nitty gritty of astral travel by exploring ways you can visualize yourself moving in space.

This will provide a solid framework that will help you to begin developing your astral body and learning to travel with it.

The first step is to understand what an astral body is and how it works. To keep it simple: we have three bodies, a physical body, an etheric or emotional body, and a mental body (some traditions include more bodies). The astral body is the easiest to form, and exists in a state which is more or less "in-between" the etheric/emotional and mental bodies. It has many properties of both, similar to a bridge between the two.

The astral body can be separated from the physical body during dreaming or meditation, but also spontaneously with people who are particularly suggestible or those who may have experienced trauma. For example, an individual who has been traumatized through childhood abuse sometimes forms an "astral" image of the perpetrator which can then be projected as a tormenting entity that stalks them in their sleep. In this case, a person may have their astral body 'separated' from their physical body with the help of the OBE.

The astral body is a dynamic element. It is like a hologram in that it can be reconstructed over and over again. Each time it is recreated, it has a slightly different focus or "density". Because of this, astral travelers are often surprised by what they see around them in the astral plane (such as different colors and vegetation), much like one might be surprised by changes in the landscape when traveling through time or space on Earth. Some have also had experiences where they run into people that they knew during their previous lives.

The astral body is very intricate and complex, much like upper-level computer programs, but it can also be broken down into more basic elements.

The "astral body" is a vague term that means the part of our mind which is between the physical body and the mental body. The mental body handles memory and thoughts, while the astral body deals with our emotions and feelings. An individual whose astral body has been damaged may find that their thoughts become clouded or they are unable to regulate their emotions when in situations where they might normally feel angry or sad.

The astral body is highly vulnerable to psychic attacks.

This is because it can be created in the blink of an eye and is not as resilient as the physical body. For example, a person who has had an OBE or has developed their astral body to a sophisticated degree may be able to exert influence over what they see or feel at different levels of consciousness, but if done during sleep they will have little control over their dreams. This is a great chance for one to become susceptible to negative entities and one should take care when visiting the astral plane during sleep.

Astral projection involves separating the astral body from the physical, as opposed to lucid dreaming which involves maintaining some form of awareness while dreaming. This means that in order to astral project, one must make sure that their mind does not become too caught up with the physical body. This is fairly easy to do, as we spend a good deal of our day-to-day lives thinking about thoughts and memories. Instead, it is much more effective to focus on your own feelings and emotions, such as those related to love or hate.

Since the astral body can be created from any element we place in it (especially from fear), it is considered a very open field to work with and should be treated carefully.

You should go through a pre-meditation exercise to relax your body and clear your mind, as suggested in the 'Pre-procedure' section.

Once you are relaxed, you can begin by imaging that you are sitting in an empty space. You will see around you a light, a fog or even just colored dots or other geometric shapes. It is important to let this develop naturally and form itself without trying to force it into something else.

As you sit in this state, you may feel yourself being pulled or it may happen on its own. Perhaps a bright white light will begin to appear from the top of your field of vision; try to notice what color it is and try to focus on how it feels.

As you drift into this state, you may feel that your eyes are shutting – this is common and usually happens when the mind relaxes enough that your body wants to take over for it. This is just part of the process. You should not fight or resist these actions as they are all completely normal, even if at first they seem unusual.

Once your eyes have closed, you may feel as though you are falling. This too is completely normal. Do not be afraid or worried about this; if you are, it may cause you to lose the state of relaxation that is required for astral projection.

As you start to fall asleep and your eyes fall shut, try to imagine yourself in a series of rooms (of increasing size), without giving names to any one of them. As your awareness becomes more sensitive, the imagery will become more vivid and real before your eyes begin to open again.

This means you have successfully astral projected. You can attempt this again any time you like, but remember to maintain the same level of concentration needed.

The majority of astral projections occur during sleep, but sometimes the mind can become distracted from sleep and the body at other times during the day. Because of this, it is important to realize that beginning an astral projection after a period of time has passed may require more effort on your part because your body may be less receptive to such activity. In this case, it is best to wait until you are in a sleeping environment before attempting your astral projection again.

After you have successfully astral projected, you will find that your mind is more clear and your emotions are more easily felt. You may also feel as though you are floating or falling downward. These sensations will dissipate after a few minutes and it is important to not attempt to re-enter an astral projection without first allowing these sensations to fade away.

Here are some things that can occur during an astral projection:

If you feel anything strange while trying to astral project, do not be afraid or worried; this is normal. Just relax and go with the feeling for a few moments before deciding how to respond to this sensation. If you do notice anything strange occur, it is best to ignore it and continue to follow your original plan.

If you have never had an OBE before, there are a few things to keep in mind when attempting this for the first time. When going through your pre-meditation exercise before going to sleep, try not to think of the physical world when you begin imagining yourself in an empty space. Instead try focusing on your own feelings and emotions while there. Do not attempt to make solid shapes out of air around you because this will only distract you from the main task at hand! When creating the feeling of falling away from physical reality, try thinking that you are just falling into nothingness. However, because you are imagining this, there is no reason to be concerned about the possibility of not being able to find your way back.

An important thing to remember is that after you have successfully astral projected, you will feel more at ease and happier than when in the physical realm. It is important to enjoy this feeling while it lasts, even if the experience is less than what you had hoped for, because it can improve over time.

SECTION FOR BELAYING ANY FEARS ONE MIGHT HAVE BEFORE YOU EVEN GET TO THE DIFFERENT METHODS

B e patient with yourself and keep practicing, and before you know it you'll be able to leave your body at will in no time!

Before you even think about going astral projecting, though, please make sure that all of your mental faculties are in check. If you don't feel emotionally or physically stable enough for this process — that's okay! Take a break from astral projection for a short period until you're ready.

Without further ado, here are a few methods you can use to achieve this state:

As you can see, the techniques are very similar between the two, with the only difference being that for the Activation Level III process, you have to focus on your breath and intent in order to levitate off of the surface. The Activation Level I technique only requires your intent.

The Processes:

The first thing is to find yourself in a dimly lit room without any windows or decorations, where there are no distractions for you.

Once you have the room ready, take your seat and close your eyes.

Start focusing on your breath and intent. Think of all the things that you want to accomplish in this lifetime and think about them again and again. Think positive thoughts!

After some time, it should occur naturally for you to levitate off of the ground. If you're having difficulty doing so, remind yourself of the things you want to accomplish in this lifetime, and how you need to be able to levitate off of the ground in order to do so.

The moment before your body levitates off of the ground for the first time, say these words: "I WILL LEAVE MY BODY AND ASCEND TO THE HEAVENS."

Think positive thoughts the entire time — don't let negative thoughts or doubts creep into your mind. You can do this!

When you have fully left your body, you will feel as if there's a balloon tied around your waist. You will see your body below you.

Feel free to levitate around the room, but it is recommended that you ascend upward as a test for your first time going out of body. Ascending upwards, you should go through the ceiling and keep ascending upwards until you reach a point where it's black. This is the void.

The reason that we recommend ascending up to the blackness of the void is because this signifies that the journey back into your body is very close — at least in comparison to if you traveled downwards or stayed where you were.

You will ascend upwards until you reach a white, bright light. This light is the door back into your body. The key is to be able to go into this light without getting sucked into it. Remember that you're not going through the light — you're going around it in order for you to return inside of your body.

Once you have circled the white light and reached your body, say "I WILL RETURN NOW," and feel yourself being pulled back down by gravity along with a feeling of relief that you returned safely. You will be all right.

And for the second time, you'll be able to leave your body! It's something you can do!"

CONCLUSION

Astral Projection is the act of the spirit or soul leaving the physical body to experience life in, and explore, other dimensions. It does not involve a journey into past lives.

Despite popular perceptions, astral projection is not an escape from reality but rather an extension of one's perception of reality beyond its third dimensional understanding. It is a means for looking at how things are interrelated rather than independent - seeing all aspects of self as well as all others without bias and prejudice. Astral projection brings about profound insights that can be helpful on many levels including self-awareness and personal growth.

Orbs are simply another manifestation in the astral dimension which can take many different forms there depending on what they represent: love, fear, hatred... many other things.

A silver cord ties the physical body, along with the astral body, to the physical vehicle. When this cord is cut, the physical body dies and disappears. It was believed to be a thin white rope which was formed at death, but more recent research has shown it to be a central magnetic pathway which connects to an energetic part of the brain; as such it is not necessary for all aspects of astral phenomena involving disconnection of a silver cord.

On Earth we experience three primary planes or dimensions: physical reality, astral reality and spiritual reality. Astral projection involves travel between these three planes of existence and thus it is called Out-of-Body Experience (OOBE).

The three planes of existence are layered, just as the earth and the atmosphere around it are layered. The astral plane is adjacent to our physical world. In fact, you are already in it right now as you read this. It simply exists at a frequency level higher than that of the visible light spectrum and is thus invisible to our eyes. However, some people can see into this plane with their psychic sight even though their physical eyes can't perceive it.

Our mind and all its faculties work on the astral plane. Although we do not have physical sensations there, we still have emotions, thoughts, ideas and perceptions as well as an inner awareness of ourselves both individually and collectively with other souls. When we go astral, we leave our physical body behind, but we continue to exist as a soul for a while.

The difference in the astral plane between people is that everybody has a different background and experiences there. This is called astral karma or lifestreaming and it is what's important here. The astral plane is a kind of mirror world of our earth and it reflects back to us what had happened on earth in our lifetime.

The astral plane is full of wise beings who are willing to help you. There are no bad or evil beings there. Just as on earth, some people are good and some people will take advantage of you. You create your own reality here just as you do on earth. However, when you project out, it is not so much for you to create your own reality as to experience the reality that already exists there for you – to learn from it, grow from it and make the necessary changes in your life if necessary.

The astral plane is a world of subtle energy; it is a kind of spiritual reality – something like the spirit world. However the astral plane is not the spirit world, it is a part of it, as is the physical dimension. The spirit world or afterlife exists prior to physical reality and beyond it. However, in some ways you could call all three planes together - earth plane, astral plane and spiritual plane - as one big universe or cosmos. Imagine what would happen if our mind was able to see truly into this whole universe. There is no end to it.

Out of body experiences (OOBEs) tend to be of the astral plane and not that of the spiritual. This means that we can learn from experience and become less ignorant as a result. More complicated are the cases when someone projects into spirit reality and interacts with souls there, but this is much rarer. When you project, it is usually for one reason only: to learn something about yourself which you need to know on your path of spiritual evolution, your own inner development.

Astral projections (also called astral travel) are often accompanied by OBEs in which some part of our pure consciousness leaves the body while maintaining an awareness that it is "out". The ability to achieve out of body experiences (OOBEs) is the result of conscious relaxation techniques, deep meditation, and an open minded state of mind.

Astral projection is a natural experience for some people. For others however it can be a spiritual development that makes them perceive the world in a very different way. This is not to be confused with psychic phenomenon however, although these can occur during OBE's and are also important to understand.

With meditation techniques experienced in India over thousands of years there has been recorded evidence that human consciousness can leave its physical form using what is known as the Astral body as opposed to its physical body during astral travel or exit projection.

In this experience the physical body is left behind, but the astral body retains awareness. This causes a 'sensor' type of consciousness that can be seen as a window between the physical and spiritual worlds. The projection of this consciousness into another time and space is usually accompanied by in-depth experiences in "the now." During these experiences it is possible for a person to be able to perceive any information they might need in order to make the right decisions at the right time. A session of this type can often be very relaxing regarding which information will manifest, but may also be quite overwhelming for some people due to its depth and intensity. A person may also find himself or herself in an altered state of consciousness for a period of time after "projecting" during the session. Thus, there can be a feeling of being very detached and disoriented during this time period, but it can often lead to very profound insights about the self and others. The result can be a person learning more about their soul nature and what type of being they are.

Many people who have experienced this form of projection feel that it has helped them become more spiritually aware. They may also feel that they have had "a visitation" from someone who is still on Earth or in one way or another has guided them in their life path.

Astral Projection is a form of lucid dreaming. Lucid dreaming can be described as the practice of having one's awareness while in the dream, guides one through the dream experience.

Lucid dreaming has been variously defined as a dream during which one is aware that he or she is dreaming and realizes that this awareness has, in fact, been present all along; it can be associated with waking consciousness. It does not necessarily entail an outer reality to be perceived by people. Psychologists have suggested that our subconscious mind sends signals to our conscious mind which make it aware we are having a Dream (Lucid Dreaming).

Astral Projection has been identified as an altered state of consciousness (ASC) where normal physical sensory input is not present. ASCs are characterized by sensory deprivation and include meditation, day dreaming, trance states and hypnagogia. ASCs have a number of psychological effects including an intense feeling of love or happiness which is often described as an "expanded state of consciousness". Some accounts describe the experience as being outside one's body, in outer space or traveling to other parts of the world and passing through walls etc. The experience may also be accompanied by out-of-body experiences (OBE's) in which some part of our pure consciousness leaves the body while maintaining an awareness that it is "out".

Unlike OBE's, where the individual has a near-permanent awareness of being unconscious, ones consciousness has fully left the body before returning in some cases. The ASC state is described as an all-pervading state of bliss and love. It is characterized by feelings of transcendence and involvement with other worldly beings. Sometimes this can be accompanied by out-of-body experiences (OBE's) in which some part of our pure consciousness leaves the body while maintaining an awareness that it is "out". Physical evidence can be obtained from a postmortem examination. Some people may recall dreams from one or more nights for several months afterward.

It is not possible to know whether a person who claims to have astral projection has actually experienced it, since nocturnal hallucinations of an astral nature are common in normal sleep. One should also note that for some people OBE's during sleep may occur regularly without hypnagogic episodes.

It should be understood that the psychology of projection and other forms of ASCs is still quite poorly understood. It seems likely that whilst they can also produce great benefits, their use by some people (e.g., in the development of self-hypnotism) can lead to serious harm.

Made in United States
Troutdale, OR
06/11/2023

10550554R00116